PRAISE FOR *ENCOUNTERS WITH POWER*

"José Luis Stevens brings us jewels of wisdom from the world's most ancient spiritual path. A brilliant and heart-warming book of personal tales of power and the journey beyond life and death. Exquisite!"

ALBERTO VILLOLDO, PHD
bestselling author of *Shaman, Healer, Sage* and *One Spirit Medicine*

"When a shaman writes an autobiography, it must be a book of many stories because the shaman's life is composed of characters, plots, adventures, misadventures, and teachings. José Luis Stevens has laid out some of the signature events of his own life in wonderful stories that are sometimes humorous, sometimes painful, but always with deep teachings about how to find spiritual power and use it ethically. As he points out, becoming powerful means leaving your comfort zone and being open to the times when things go wrong as well as right. It is through personal stories that we receive from Spirit the gifts of insight and wisdom, and through José's stories, you will receive those gifts."

TOM COWAN
author of *Fire in the Head* and *Yearning for the Wind*

"José Luis Stevens uses the shamanic art of teaching through storytelling to share his depth of wisdom and knowledge with us. I was deeply touched by his remarkable stories and how the lessons he learned apply to all of us as we learn how to stand in our power. José's willingness to be so authentic and vulnerable is part of the magic of *Encounters with Power*. This book is filled with demonstrations of how we can quest for power, find balance, and discover our authentic self. I was fully engaged while reading *Encounters with Power* and feel it is an important book for the times we live in."

SANDRA INGERMAN, MA
author of *The Shamanic Journey: A Beginner's Guide* and *Walking in Light*

"José Luis Stevens is an accomplished writer and storyteller who shares his own tales of power."

"A seasoned shamanic teacher and consummate ceremonialist, José Luis Stevens's gift of storytelling is on a par with the soul-illuminating tales spoken by tribal wisdom keepers of time immemorial. A journey of personal revelation, inspired evolution, and enlightened right action, *Encounters with Power* will undoubtedly prove to be a classic in the fields of neo-shamanism and contemporary ethnospiritual inquiry. All earnest navigators of non-ordinary human consciousness will find this book to be an honest, transparent narrative on the inherent perils and pitfalls of seeking shamanic power—a raw tale of embarking upon a path of service nurtured by the sanity found in self-liberation. On a more global scale, I'm convinced the wonderfully-articulated perennial wisdom within this beautifully written book shall serve to further catalyze the cross-cultural democratization of shamanism as a collective path of earth-centered spiritual living. In essence, I believe all who read *Encounters with Power* will gain deeper insight into their own personal struggles and challenges as vital preparation to walk more gently and lovingly, with seven-generation healing service in heart, as sacred passerby upon our beloved Gaia-Pachamama. Highly recommended!"

"For thousands of years, our ancestors shared teachings through an oral tradition of storytelling. In *Encounters with Power*, we have the honor of sitting around a timeless fire with an elder and ingesting the experiences of a lifetime of potent, transformative wisdom stories. Drink deep of this much needed draught of medicine words."

HEATHERASH AMARA
author of *Warrior Goddess Training*

"José Luis Stevens is a master storyteller. Reading *Encounters with Power*, we get inside the stories, we feel the emotions and anticipations. In telling his personal adventures, José displays much humility and authenticity, which is personal power. Good stories, even personal ones, are collective. These stories teach us in a way that is whole. This is a marvelous book, lots of fun to read, hard to put down, and the teachings you receive almost effortlessly seem meant for you. I recommend it."

CLAUDE PONCELET, PHD
author of *The Shaman Within*

"José Luis Stevens's engaging accounts of his spiritual unfolding reveal the excitement of the travels, as well as the travails that may transpire, when we walk the spiritual path in search of "encounters with power." There is much teaching and knowledge in his stories that may bring us into connection with our inner chief—the leader within each of us who takes responsibility for doing what needs to be done—as well as for creating abundance through our relationship with nature."

HANK WESSELMAN, PHD
anthropologist and author of the *Spiritwalker* trilogy,
the award-winning *Awakening to the Spirit World*
(with Sandra Ingerman), *The Bowl of Light*, and
The Re-Enchantment: A Shamanic Path to a Life of Wonder

"True to ancient shamanic traditions, José Luis Stevens's riveting personal stories are profound teachings. There is no other way to teach the mystery unless you experience it through gratitude, love, and awe. I highly recommend this courageous book by a man in search of power, self-realization, and awakening."

ITZHAK BEERY
author *The Gift of Shamanism: Visionary Power, Ayahuasca Dreams, and Journeys to the Other Realms*; publisher of ShamanPortal.com

"*Encounters with Power* is a wonderful blend of story, instruction, and advice. It is written in a style that is clear, warm, and comfortable. While reading it, we become villagers sharing the heart of the storyteller through the artistry of the writer. The conversation between José and his mother on her deathbed is priceless. His Map of the Four Axes helps us to position ourselves to receive the blessings available in every direction. He shows us how to become the Artist, the Healer, the Warrior, and the Teacher. For the devotees of African diaspora traditions, this work can be understood as a shamanic interpretation of the powers of Eshu Yangi, the deity who guides us on the many paths between heaven and earth. Savor it."

LUISAH TEISH
author of *Jambalaya: The Natural Woman's Book of Personal Charms and Practical Rituals*

"An extraordinary read! José is a master storyteller, each story a lesson in itself. A must-read for those interested in evolving on their shamanic path."

JAMES ENDREDY
author of *Teachings of the Peyote Shamans: The Five Points of Attention* and *Advanced Autogenic Training and Primal Awareness: Techniques for Wellness, Deeper Connection to Nature, and Higher Consciousness*

ENCOUNTERS
WITH
POWER

ALSO BY JOSÉ LUIS STEVENS

Awaken the Inner Shaman: A Guide to the Power Path of the Heart

The Power Path: The Shaman's Way to Success in Business and Life

Praying with Power:
How to Use Ancient Shamanic Techniques to Gain Maximum
Spiritual Benefit and Extraordinary Results Through Prayer

Secrets of Shamanism: Tapping the Spirit Power Within You

Transforming Your Dragons:
How to Turn Fear Patterns into Personal Power

Sections by José Luis Stevens in Sandra Ingerman
and Hank Wesselman's *Awakening to the Spirit World:*
The Shamanic Path of Direct Revelation

Ebook Series: *The Personessence System for Understanding People*
(available at thepowerpath.com)

- *Introduction to the Personessence System*
- *The Seven Archetypal Roles: Primary Way of Being*
- *The Seven Goals and the Seven Modes: Primary Motivation*
  and Primary Approach
- *The Seven Attitudes: Primary Perspective*
- *The Seven Obstacles: Primary Fear Patterns*
- *The Seven Centers: Primary Reaction Centers and*
  Communication Styles
- *The Nine Needs: Primary Requirements for Balance*
- *The Seven States of Perception: Primary Values*
- *Spiritual and Cosmological Guide to the Personessence System*

JOSÉ LUIS STEVENS, PhD

ENCOUNTERS
WITH
POWER

Adventures and Misadventures
on the Shamanic Path of Healing

BOULDER, COLORADO

Sounds True
Boulder, CO 80306

Published 2017

Cover design by Jennifer Miles
Book design by Beth Skelley

Printed in Canada

Library of Congress Cataloging-in-Publication Data

Names: Stevens, José, author.
Title: Encounters with power : adventures and misadventures on the
Shamanic path of healing / José Luis Stevens, PhD.
Description: Boulder, CO : Sounds True, Inc., [2017]
Identifiers: LCCN 2016018939 (print) | LCCN 2016037476 (ebook) |
  ISBN 9781622037933 | ISBN 9781622037940 (ebook)
Subjects: LCSH: Shamanism.
Classification: LCC BF1611 .S7978 2017 (print) | LCC BF1611 (ebook) |
  DDC 201/.44—dc23
LC record available at https://lccn.loc.gov/2016018939

10 9 8 7 6 5 4 3 2 1

To all of my teachers on these encounters with power,
particularly the teachers willing to play the villains
leading to my most powerful lessons.

And to my wonderful shamanic mentors who have transitioned:
Angeles Arrien, Guadalupe Candelario, and Herlinda Alverez.

CONTENTS

PART III Action—Chief-Warrior

INTRODUCTION

Tell us a story, José! Tell us a story!

For years around the campfires of my various shamanic programs, I have been asked to tell my stories: stories of magic, adventure, and outrageous situations—stories with teachings about the shamanic way. The best of them, and the ones my listeners often enjoy most, are about misadventures or times when I was presented with situations that seemed impossible.

Now that I am an elder teacher, I figure it's time to write some of these stories down. What you are about to read is not strictly an autobiography, but these are true stories from my life, or stories that people I encountered in my wanderings told to me. Every time I tell one of them it is a little different, and certainly, other individuals who were present for these events might remember them differently. What matters is that I lived these experiences and saw and felt them in light of what I was learning at the time.

The theme of all the stories in this book is "encounters with power." Shamanically speaking, life is all about becoming more powerful: learning to acquire power, store it, seal it in, and express it when needed. A single tree demonstrates power as it explodes from the seed and seeks the sunlight above. A hawk expresses power as it pecks its way out of the egg, screams for food, and one day takes that flying leap out of the nest into the sky. Learning about power is also a main theme for human beings on this planet. Most of our world problems would be solved if we learned our lessons about power well, so perhaps reading these stories will help you on your quest for power, for learning, and for your application to and influence on the big picture.

Life is filled with initiations: tests to see if we are ready for more power. Many of these tests tend to be brutal, ruthless, or harsh. They get our attention, for sure. We could easily conclude from the nature of these tests that we are powerless and should give up. On the other hand, we can rise to the occasion and find ways to become powerful enough to prove otherwise.

WHAT IS AN ENCOUNTER WITH POWER?

An encounter with power is different for each person. For me, the experience could be anywhere from highly interesting to terrifying. Or I might simply find it hugely entertaining.

Power exists everywhere, so an encounter with power can happen in any environment. As I have written in other books—especially in *The Power Path: The Shaman's Way to Success in Business and Life*—power is not something you can own. It is like the air you breathe. You meet it, breathe it in, take sustenance from it, and then release it. Little by little you accumulate its benefits, and over time you become more powerful. In itself, power is neutral, but you can give it a dark spin through ignorance, lack of respect, or ill intent. Power can destroy you or it can raise you up by teaching and nourishing you.

I intend for these stories to teach you how best to approach power. As you will clearly understand when you read them, I have not yet mastered power, but I have learned a few things you may find helpful on your own quest for mastery.

Although I have had the good fortune to lead an amazingly adventurous life, my stories are still within the range of most people's experience. When I read the Carlos Castaneda books many years ago, I was mesmerized, but they seemed so far out there that I could not imagine experiencing such things myself.

For the most part, my stories are not like those. Unlike Castaneda, I haven't suddenly found myself wandering around on different planets or confronting drooling monsters the size of houses. In this lifetime my task is to be a bridge person, a pivotal facilitator, and if I am too far out there I could not do that very well. Nevertheless, if you look at reality conventionally, my stories are filled with amazing synchronicities and unlikely happenings.

I have at times included the real names of my teachers, people such as Guadalupe, Enrique, and Herlinda. I have changed other names either by request or to avoid harming the reputation of someone I had an unpleasant incident with. In some cases I have changed the exact locations of certain events, again to honor individuals' privacy or to protect them from being tracked down by eager adventurers. In a couple of cases I altered the timing of events to make it easier to tell the story. However, rest assured that I have included nothing that did not actually happen. I hope you enjoy these uncommon adventures and will let them teach you as if you are experiencing them yourself.

HOW THIS BOOK IS ORGANIZED
The Map of the Four Axes

A challenge I had in compiling these stories was to group widely disparate happenings into like themes. I tried organizing them by chronology, location, and so on but finally settled on grouping them according to a unique map of shamans' specialties that I call the Map of the Four Axes. I have always loved and studied maps of all kinds, and on the shamanic path I have found some of the best ancient maps in the world—the medicine wheel and the tree of life, among others. Along the way I discovered another map that fits the shamanic model perfectly, and ultimately I organized these stories to align with it, both to share the map with you and to help you navigate the world from shamanic viewpoints.

If you are not familiar with shamanism, it is the world's most ancient spiritual path, a practical approach to life that helped humankind survive from its earliest appearance on the planet. I have found it wonderfully helpful in clarifying the meaning of so many of my life experiences.

About the Map

This powerful map is really quite simple. It has no traditional given name, and like so many extremely valuable bits of ancient wisdom, it is unfamiliar to most people, having been passed down orally for many centuries, mostly in secret. Every once in a while it surfaces to help humankind out in a time of crisis—such as now. Bear in mind that it can map practically anything you want it to.

The map displays the four axes that hold this universe together, the four ways that energy can travel toward within this three-dimensional universe. These axes are Expression, Inspiration, Action, and Assimilation. The best method to display these axes is by depicting a wagon wheel with three axes crossing the wheel like spokes. In the middle is a hub through which another axis goes horizontally.

The Four Ways

The way of Expression is radiant like the sun, with energy traveling outward in every direction. Expression allows things to be revealed, seen, heard, touched, and experienced.

The way of Inspiration is upward, making available that which was hidden, raising it so we can rise up on our evolutionary path.

The way of Action is forward, accounting for evolution, progress, and productivity.

The way of Assimilation is inward; it allows information to be absorbed, integrated, accommodated, or adapted to.

Three of the axes have two aspects and one is solo, making up seven aspects in all. The seven aspects as they relate to the shamanic path are as follows: In the Expression axis are the Storyteller and the Artist; in the Inspiration axis are the Ceremonialist and the Healer; in the Action axis are the Warrior and the Chief; and in the Assimilation axis is the teacher/student, or Man/Woman of Knowledge. The Assimilation axis is in the middle of the circle and draws from each of the other axes. Together, these

Map of The Seven Shamanic Specialties

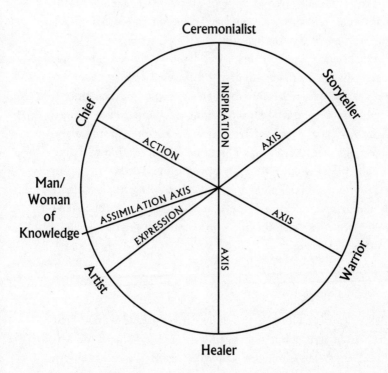

are the seven specialties of the shaman. Every shaman should have training in each category but typically becomes a specialist in one.

All people in cultures that practice shamanism—which is to say most indigenous cultures—express themselves through art. They sing, dance, make sacred objects, create altars, and so on. The shamans among them also become adept at telling teaching stories. They are also trained in the healing arts and can conduct many different ceremonies; lift people out of misery, pain, and suffering; and provide people with transformative experiences. As trained warriors, all shamans do battle with demons, whether they take the form of physical illness, mental problems, or internal conflicts. Shamans are capable leaders of their tribe or kingdom and take responsibility for their well-being. Ultimately, with time and experience, all shamans become women and men of great knowledge and wisdom.

In keeping with the map, this book is divided into three parts, one for each of the first three axes: Expression, Inspiration, and Action. Within each part at the end of each story is a postscript commentary about some of the lessons I learned from my experiences. I have also included some exercises and questions that I hope you will find helpful in relation to them.

You might wonder what happened to the fourth axis, Assimilation—The Man/Woman of Knowledge. That part, dear reader, is the axis you occupy—the one acquiring knowledge—and that I occupy as well, the one who assimilated these experiences as they happened.

¤

Before I turn you loose to travel these pages, let me say that these stories represent a body of experiences that have made me who I am: a good psychologist, a spiritual teacher, a ceremonialist, husband, father, and grandpa—in short, a wise fool. I am happy with who I am, a partner in spirit; what I am, fully human; and how I choose to serve in this life as a teacher. There are more adventures to come, more mistakes, more learning, more riches in the blessings of being alive and present. In the meantime, I am pleased to offer you some stories of a lifetime—my lifetime to date. Enjoy!

PART I

EXPRESSION
Storyteller-Artist

The stories in part I best fit under the category of expression—the storyteller and artist. While each story in this book has elements of all the aspects of the shamanic map, the ones you will read in this section truly are tales of encounters with power and are the best examples of pure expression. They teach by going to many places, by shining light on all aspects of an experience.

The shaman storyteller teaches by telling riveting stories, funny stories, stories that carry lessons. The storyteller has to make the tales come alive, to get listeners on the edge of their seats, to fascinate and entertain them. Shaman storytellers must believe in their own stories, know them from the inside out, and sell them to a crowd that always wants more. They must also leave their stories with a bit of mystery, an aspect of the unknown that allows room for listeners to come up with their own understandings, lessons, and realizations.

For the artist shaman, living is an art, learning is an art, and all art can be expressed in myriad ways: through song, dance, and symbolic forms. This expresses to the people what cannot always be said in words.

1

THE POWER OF PROPHECY

India and the
Life-Changing Reading

In July 1976 I quit my job as a psychiatric social worker at Napa State Hospital in Northern California, a foreboding collection of institutional-green concrete buildings with few windows. I had put in my two years of postgraduate work to gain enough hours to be licensed in the state of California as an independent practitioner. Functioning as the assistant ward administrator on an adolescent locked unit, I carried heavy skeleton keys that I used to lock myself into the ward as if I were going to prison every day. This unit included both psychotic teenagers and seriously sociopathic young people who were in the hospital for arson, prostitution, violence, drug dealing, murdering their parents and barbecuing them in the backyard, killing their siblings, and hijacking a jet.

Ronald Reagan had mandated a state hiring freeze during his tenure as governor, cutting the budget for mental health care and turning out thousands of mentally unstable people onto the streets—an unconscionable cost-cutting act that was conveniently forgotten during his presidency. The result on my ward was that as staff left through attrition, they were not replaced.

The policy of the hospital was that a male staff member had to be present on the ward at all times to restrain violent patients. Eventually I became that one man, although I had never been trained to restrain anyone. I was not a psychiatric technician but rather a liaison between kids, parents, schools, probation officers, and the court system. Already, one male staff member had been permanently disabled by a violent six-foot-two eighteen-year-old who put him in the hospital. I figured it was only a matter of time until it was my turn.

At one point the hospital director shuffled staff and sent me to work on a ward with profoundly developmentally disabled children. I had no heart for this work, so when my two years were up I followed my supervisor's advice and quit. "Get in, get your training, and get out," she had told me, "or you'll become a lifer." "Lifers" were staff who were hard to distinguish from the patients, except that they had a set of keys and a salary.

On the day I quit I felt such relief—like the weight of ages had lifted from my shoulders. I was a free man, and I was determined to make the most of it. My relationship with Lena had been developing from housemates to boy- and girlfriend, but in a bold and risky move I stored my belongings and booked myself a flight to Hong Kong. I would embark on this adventure solo and with no plans to return at any particular point. I was twenty-eight, in my Saturn return, and for years I had wanted to see Asia, India, and Nepal. After a short visit to Hong Kong and a mind-blowing week in Thailand, I headed for my primary destination, India, where the spiritual comingled with the ordinary every day. I could hardly wait.

INDIA

I had just left northern Thailand and my world had already been rocked by events beyond my comprehension, including witnessing a unique Buddhist ceremony where dancers stabbed themselves repeatedly with steel swords and suffered no injury. After flying for hours over green jungle with watercourses snaking into the distance below me, the plane left land for the ocean. Nothing could have prepared me for the experience of landing at the Delhi airport in northern India that fall after my twenty-eighth birthday.

The Vietnam War had recently ended and my thoughts were heavy with what had transpired there, just to the east of where I was now flying. I thought about friends who had died there and Jerry, the one who returned without a face. I had gone to see him at the VA hospital in San Diego and was forever sickened by what I saw. A man I had known and liked lay in a hospital bed with a small tube running out of a hole in the side of what used to be a mouth. His eyes and nose were gone. There were no identifiable features left on his face. His body was covered with lurid red scars where surgeons had removed shrapnel. Jerry had lived just down the hall of my college dorm, a friendly, handsome guy full of energy and vitality. We all knew he had a military dad who pressured him to "be a man," join the Marines as he had, and go fight the enemies of the United States in Vietnam. That was in 1966 when the war was heating up. We students already knew it was about oil, competition, and ideologies, a serious waste of lives and money.

We all talked about how wrong the war was, so we were shocked the day Jerry went off to join the Marines. His dad's pressure had finally overpowered him and he wanted so much to prove himself to his father. We were horrified and very concerned for him. Three months later he had been torn to pieces by a mortar that blew up in his face and I was visiting him in the hospital. Perhaps his father was proud, I thought, now that Jerry had come home a grossly disabled veteran.

As I flew toward India, I thought about Richard Nixon announcing the end of college exemptions from the draft and about watching the lottery on television with my college buddies. My birth date came up number 25, so low that I was certain to be drafted within a couple of months. We all got drunk that night. Two months later I was in the Oakland Induction Center standing naked in a long line of young guys who had received draft notices. Meanwhile, Vietnam had become carnage. Thousands of young men were dying over there and the war was only escalating. It was crystal clear to us that the war was a serious miscalculation and a mistake of horrific proportions, and only the administration wasn't getting it yet.

I had made plans to go to Canada if I passed the medical portion of the exam. I could not in good conscience kill people in a war I did not believe in. In fact, having been a soldier many times in past lives, I had had enough of war. I knew I had sent many men to their deaths in other times and places when I was a younger soul. War had never solved anything, and killing was not in my nature anymore. Fortunately, with heavy help from Spirit, I failed the medical exam and was given a permanent 1-Y status, meaning that I would only be drafted in a national emergency. As it turned out, they did not want someone with a history of childhood eczema scrambling around in the jungles of Vietnam. I did not have to go to Canada after all, and I could go on to more productive endeavors. As I walked out of that induction center onto the noisy Oakland street, I felt a huge and tearful relief. I was twenty years old and very happy to be alive.

Now, a decade later as I flew toward the exotic destination of India, I realized why I had not gone to Vietnam. There were other more important things to do with my life. I had a destiny and it was unfolding before my eyes.

A landscape covered with a thick curtain of brown air appeared on the horizon, and I felt a rush of exhilaration. As I deplaned in the dusk, that hot brown air hit me like a wall, an oven thick with smoke and grit. The smells of burning charcoal and dung hung heavy in the air, tugging at a distant memory. *It was all so familiar.* I took a wild taxi ride from the airport, with incessant honking, oxcarts, bicycles, scooters, brown women dressed in saris with brass pots on their heads, and rumbling trucks. A painted elephant lent an unreal quality to the ancient chaos that is India. Fresh from the mysteries of Thailand, I was about to begin an adventure that would propel my growth to the breaking point.

If I had known then what I was in for, perhaps I would not have had the courage to go to India, but innocence is the fuel of adventure. Shortly after arriving, I became so ill I nearly died. I was lodged in a government guesthouse beside a railway station in an unknown village. Alone and gripped by fever in a hot, dark, windowless room with a rotating fan, all I could do was lie there and hallucinate. For four days, weakened by high fever, dysentery, and vomiting, I couldn't get out of bed. No one knew where I was, I had no way of contacting anyone, and I couldn't even get to a doctor because I was too sick to leave my room. Eventually the fever broke and I spewed thick green scum for several days before I was able to resume my travels.

I gradually made my way to Varanasi, also known as Banares, which is located on the banks of the Ganges River. Varanasi is the holiest of Indian cities and the sacred place where Hindus bring their dead and dying. At the river's edge were *ghats*—stone steps leading down to the river—upon which pyres towered with flames burning corpses to ash. As I made my way through the twisted streets, I glimpsed an unforgettable sight: a three-wheeled pedicab with a corpse propped up in the passenger's seat, the body wrapped in cotton strips like a mummy. The unconcerned driver was calmly pedaling the cab down to the burning ghats.

Following the cab, I made my way down to the river's edge to view the throngs bathing beside the temples that lined the shore. I watched the rituals of the Hindu priests and the fires consuming the corpses. Day after day I visited this fascinating place, transfixed by the colorful but morbid display. I watched men from the untouchable class dive for gold teeth fillings, coins, and bits of valuables they could glean from the ashes dumped into the brackish waters of the Ganges. Skulls, hands, feet, and ribcages glowed in the coals of pyres as priests chanted, bells rang, and clouds of incense billowed skyward. Many years later I would learn that watching the burning of the dead was a Hindu practice of the highest order.

Before I left the United States, a psychiatrist friend gave me the name of a professor of Ayurvedic medicine at the world-renowned Banares Hindu University in Varanasi. I was to look up the psychiatrist's colleague, Harish Shukla, and say hello. I tracked down the professor and the serious-looking older gentleman immediately invited me to his home, an impressive two-story structure on a major street. We spoke for many hours about philosophy, the nature of reality, and Hindu beliefs, and he invited me to return the next day for more discussions. I did, and again we engaged in animated talks for most of the day.

He took pains to point out that our thoughts and intentions manipulate reality on a minute-by-minute basis. He explained at length how we each create our own reality in this fashion and that it is our individual responsibility to control our thoughts and fantasies, lest we inadvertently create our worst fears instead of what we truly want. I found that his explanations were in alignment with the supernatural events I had witnessed on my recent visit to Thailand—but they were dramatically different from the nature of reality I had been taught in my Catholic upbringing.

These talks were magical, and I marveled at how fortunate I was to be having them. I considered the fact that I had created this whole trip from my intent and that it was not simply a random set of events I was reacting to. I played with the idea that I was meant to meet this professor and that perhaps we had a deeper relationship than I had considered at first. He certainly had an impact on my whole outlook on life.

CONVERSATIONS WITH DR. SHUKLA

Dr. Shukla, a yogi himself, regaled me with philosophical observations and stories about his guru, who he said could raise people from the dead and appear anywhere at will, and who had announced his own death beforehand. One time Dr. Shukla asked his guru to show him the great light of the source. His guru told him he was not ready but showed him anyway by producing a powerful sound vibration. Dr. Shukla told me he was so terrified by it that he ran screaming into the night, tripped, and hurt himself. He went on to explain that the body-mind must be prepared for this vibration or the energy from the blast can be deadly. He said,

> How can a two-horsepower motor handle ten thousand volts? The average man is merely a beast, but we are capable of being divine. Only a few make it during their lifetime. We must accept our violence, competitiveness, irritation, and suffering and then go beyond it to the next higher mind-set that ultimately includes none of them. We are everything and nothing. As men we must slave to increase our power and divinity.

He then explained that there is an upsurge in mental suffering when one searches deeply within and that this is natural.

"The more I read Gandhi's book on peace," he noted, "the more I realized violence was within me. The obstacles within me began to rear their heads."

Dr. Shukla told me life was like ordering food for a meal but we only remember the very last thing we ordered:

A man may order bread but then forgets and orders fruit, meat, cheese, and coffee and then whisky. Then he notices all of them on the table in front of him and doesn't know what to do because he doesn't remember that he ordered all these things and some of them are contradictory, like coffee and whisky. He then becomes upset and blames the waiter. However, he can laugh, select what he wants, and give the rest away.

After some tea, the lessons resumed:

The physical world is experiential because it arises from a state of resistance. It has to pretend to be "not Spirit" or separate. Our bodies arise out of this resistance and therefore we suffer in them. But this is not bad and we need not suffer. All we need to do is remember that we are Spirit and that all separateness is merely an illusion. In this way we come out of resistance to the divine. People in a great state of resistance are more subject to gravity because, in a way, they have more material mass. They are depressed and bent over from the increased gravitational pull. We must grow light so that gravity exerts less force upon us. Then we will step lively and our posture will be straight.

Man is limited by his belief systems. Thus, a man who believes only in a heaven or hell is limited to expand only within this framework. It is necessary to create a belief system that is expansive enough to include every possibility, known and unknown. In this way we short-circuit the limitation of the belief system that ego seems to need in order to operate. This is the quantum leap out of ego back to godhead, or Spirit. This is the biggest math set of all.

At this point I was deeply emotional and had my fill of fascinating things to consider. Then at the perfect moment Dr. Shukla's son, Anil, a handsome young man in his early twenties, arrived. After we made introductions, Dr. Shukla excused himself for a few minutes and the conversation began anew with Anil. He spoke very good English, like his father. I learned that he was an astrologer with degrees in math, physics, and chemistry, and that he was also a whiz at chess.

Anil said, with a hint of warning in his voice, "Varanasi is a place of power. It was founded on coordinates that are perfectly adjusted, making it the perfect place to create matter out of thought. One must be careful what one desires because consequences and conditions can occur that were not anticipated."

To illustrate, he told me that his father once took pity on an old woman with tuberculosis of the joints. He laid his hands on her and healed her overnight, but soon the daughter of his guru came down with tuberculosis of the jaw because someone had to take up the slack. Then Anil told me more about his father. At his guru's touch he went into a blissful state that lasted for a full year. This became too much for him to handle because he couldn't get anything done, so he asked his guru to remove the state—which he did with a single touch.

After several days of very interesting discussions, the professor proposed that I meet Ananda, the son of the family's former guru who had become the family's spiritual guide after the guru passed. First Dr. Shukla showed me a photograph of their late guru. I saw a man in a loincloth sitting in lotus position with a shock of white hair and blazing eyes that seemed to penetrate right into my soul. It was unnerving and it frightened me not a little. I felt relieved that I was going to meet his son instead, though I was still nervous about it. Then the professor began to tell me some stories about Ananda.

He explained that when Ananda was a child he once warned him about a tragedy that ultimately came to pass. In that part of India are many poisonous snakes and people die from their bites every year. As the professor was leaving for work one morning, Ananda stopped him and said only this: "The snakes are angry today." Not understanding the meaning of this, the professor continued on to work without a second thought. When he returned home at the end of the day, he found the household weeping and his two-year-old daughter laid out in bed, dead, fatally bitten by a cobra that had slithered from under the house. Only then did Dr. Shukla remember the young guru's words.

After several more stories of this nature, I was both more intrigued and even more nervous about the meeting, yet I was especially excited by the fact that Ananda was going to give me a life reading. He asked me for my birth date and time of birth, which, fortunately, I knew by memory.

The next day at the appointed time, I walked to the professor's house in the baking heat of Varanasi's desert sun. I expected to find a man in a loincloth, so I was stunned to meet a man who appeared to be in his thirties dressed in a three-piece black suit and wearing black leather shoes. He sat in the professor's living room and spoke in crisp Hindi while Anil acted as translator. Without further ado, he asked to see my palms, which I readily showed him. He studied them for a few minutes and consulted some notes he had with him. Then he began to speak swiftly and assuredly.

"This is your life," he said, and began to tell me about my life from birth onward. He said that three people were present at my birth and proceeded to describe my family and what life had been like while I was growing up. He said I had been through many difficulties and was not understood as a child. I could readily verify what he was telling me. He went on to tell me I had been involved in social service work (remember, I was a psychiatric social worker) and that I was not married but soon would be. He described the woman I would marry, who bore a great resemblance to Lena, and then announced that I would have two children: a daughter who would be born in 1980, four years hence, and then a son who would be born in 1982. He went on and on describing my future, and as he did so I became more and more uneasy. He described great difficulties and many amazingly positive things as well. He said I would become a writer and make a specific contribution through my writing work.

He told me how long I would live, and then Anil said, "He didn't want me to tell you this but I'll tell you anyway. He said you will die from falling from a very high place and that a woman will push you."

This was just too much information. I did not want to hear it and yet once it was said it was too late—I was stuck with this terribly frightful image. Then he told me that in three days I would meet a powerful spiritual man who would greatly affect my life. With this statement he wrapped up the meeting, which had lasted about two hours. By this time I was no longer the same person I had been at the beginning of the reading. I felt as if I had grown older by twenty years. My stomach was churning, and I couldn't seem to get enough air to breathe. I was on the verge of a full-on panic attack.

It was way more than I had been prepared to hear. My thoughts were like a freeway filled with cars speeding out of control. After some farewells, I staggered out into the blazing sun and headed for the government guesthouse, where I lay down on the bed and sobbed my heart out, so traumatized I did not know what to think. The fact that he could describe my life thus far with such accuracy gave him enormous credibility. Was fate a fact? Were these things all destined to happen as he said, or did I have free will? Could I change the outcome? He had told me a couple of times that maybe I could, and that seemed to indicate that I had wiggle room. I desperately clung to this thread. And after all, Dr. Shukla had said that we create our own reality with our hopes and fears. But how could I now banish these thoughts from my mind? Around and around I obsessed until, in the wee hours of the morning, I fell asleep, exhausted.

The next day I had to plot a course of action. A part of me felt I had bitten off more than I could chew, and like a scared little kid I wanted to board a plane for home. I had no itinerary, yet there were many things I wanted to see and do. I was also determined to prove the guru wrong in order to *ensure* that I had free will. I created a plan to board a train for Madras (renamed Chennai in 1996) and then Pondicherry on the southeastern coast, a "tranquil French resort," as my tattered guidebook described it. I would hole up there for several days and avoid all meetings with people.

Standing on the platform waiting for the train, I was an emotional mess. I had no one to talk to and was extremely traumatized. I tried to think of everything I had learned in my professional training to help me cope with my mental and emotional crisis. It helped some. And as the train trundled slowly down to Madras, the scenery was so varied and interesting that I was able to distract myself from my fears.

Eventually I arrived in Pondicherry and booked a nice room in a comfortable French colonial hotel. Aah! I would hide out here. Yet I had nothing to read, and if I was going to stay here I needed reading material. In my guidebook I read about a local ashram near town that had a bookstore where I could pick up some books in English to while away the hours. The ashram had been built by a man named Sri Aurobindo, someone I knew nothing about at that time. I bought several books he had written, took them back to my hotel room, and began to read. They had titles like *The Life Divine*, *The Future Evolution of Man*, *The Human Cycle*, *The Destiny of the Body*, and *The Adventure of Consciousness*. I bought these books figuring that after reading them I would leave them behind in order to lighten my load. Little did I know I would carry them all in my backpack for months before returning to the States with them.

I read for many hours each day, hardly leaving my hotel room. I had discovered a fascinating philosophy in these pages. Then it slowly dawned on me that I had indeed met a great spiritual leader who was influencing my entire way of thinking through his writing. Although this realization horrified me because it proved the guru right, I also gained much solace through the writings. I learned that there was a much greater spiritual essence within me that did not need to worry about what would happen to my body in this life. So the guru had been right again, but in his accuracy there was also redemption for me.

As the years passed, many of the events Ananda predicted came to pass. I did indeed marry Lena, the woman he described, and my children were born exactly in the order and in the years he predicted, despite the fact that we were using various forms of birth control both times. I did become a writer and have indeed led an amazing life as he predicted. In the form of Guadalupe, my shaman teacher, I did find an older man who was like a father to me and who taught me much about life. I did meet an older woman named Beth Miller who helped me by introducing me to many influential and famous people and promoted me to my great benefit.

Yet some things did not come to pass. I did not become an importer and exporter of goods, but instead of books and shamans. I never owned a farm, but instead bought wilderness land for retreats and seminars. So I learned that although some events were indeed set in stone, I have free will to alter the course of my life. And yet I chose these destined events at a much deeper level, so there is nothing to worry about. My life is in excellent hands—and who am I to try to resist that?

As I write this, I am some years past the age when Ananda said I would die. I do not know how many years I have left, but I am very grateful for each hour, day, week, and year I am blessed with. He did say that I would have a long life, "but not too long," he added wryly. Becoming decrepit is not always a good thing and that is okay with me. I get what he meant; I just don't want to be stupid about my life. After I am dead and with my guides, I will have to go over it all with chagrin, looking at all the things I should have realized, done, and not done. I would prefer to realize them now when I am in my body. Then I can die with a smile on my face and enjoy the passage home.

¤

Although this next part of the story occurs many years later, I am skipping ahead to the mid-1990s after I moved from Berkeley, California, to Santa Fe, New Mexico. In this part of the story Lena and I were married and had two wonderful children, Anna, a teenager, and Carlos, a preteen. I had begun developing a course for people in the business world based on my book *Transforming Your Dragons: How to Turn Fear Patterns into Personal Power*. The idea was to expose businesspeople to techniques and exercises that would help them confront their fears and overcome them. I had been speaking to my friend and colleague Laurie Skreslet, a strong and powerful warrior with an inquiring mind and deep spiritual insight, and the first Canadian to summit Mount Everest. At the time, Laurie worked as a mountain guide and was on the professional speaking circuit, as he is to this day. Later I would climb Mount Aconcagua with him, but that is an altogether different story I will tell elsewhere in this book.

Laurie was interested in teaching the rock climbing aspect of the course. I had introduced him to another friend, Jan McNeal, an attractive blonde woman in her thirties and a veteran skydiving instructor who held a number of world records for women skydivers. She was a real pro, with more than fifteen hundred jumps to her credit. She was interested in doing the skydiving aspect of the course. I had met Jan in a psychology course I was teaching at JFK University in the San Francisco Bay Area. A slight complication was that Jan and I had an attraction for each other, both of us being scholars and sharing a lot of past-life history. Being married, I realized this was not tenable, so I introduced her to Laurie. I figured she would find him attractive, and to my relief they started an affair. Problem solved from my end.

The plan was that Lena and I would present the information from *Transforming Your Dragons* for the academic part of the course. Our feeling was that this would be a dynamic course integrating the best of our knowledge about confronting fear and becoming more powerful. We were very excited about the project and had drawn up some brochures and marketing materials to generate interest in the class. Then Jan pointed out that it would not be proper to offer the course unless all of us had gone through it ourselves. She was absolutely right. This meant that I had to do a tandem jump with her to get the experience of skydiving, and also do some rock climbing with Laurie. This sounded reasonable to me but nevertheless brought up my fears of jumping out of an airplane, an experience I had always wanted to have—but always managed to put off for later.

To complicate matters, I remembered what Ananda had warned me about many years before: that I would die falling from a high place and a woman would push me. Even though he had also predicted other events that had never come about, these words haunted me. Still, I was determined to go ahead. I did not want to give power to his words, and I was intent on choosing my own course with maximum freedom.

I booked a date with Jan to do a tandem jump at Belen, a site in the desert terrain south of Albuquerque and not a long drive from my home in Santa Fe. As the date neared, I actually got more and more excited about the jump. It so happened that a shaman from Peru was visiting us and had offered to do an ayahuasca ceremony for Lena and me and a few of our friends. Having done this a number of times before, I readily agreed, believing that it would be an excellent way to prepare for the jump.

In the wee hours of the morning, I was deep in a meditative state when a strange set of visions came to me with absolute clarity. First I saw a medieval knight in armor laid out on a stone slab. His arms were crossed over his chest, his hands grasping the handle of his long sword, which was pointing downward in the position of burial. He was clearly dead and a woman nearby was wailing at her loss. It became clear to me—I can't tell you how—that I was the knight and the woman was my son, Carlos, who was mourning my loss. I heard the words "He lost you once already. Don't make him lose you again." I clearly saw that I had witnessed a past-life scenario in which I was married to a woman who was Carlos in this life.

Following this realization I was immediately greeted with the heart-stopping 3-D vision of Jan and myself hurtling out of the plane and downward toward the ground. We fell at a great speed, and when she pulled the cord for the chute to open, it did not. She then pulled the reserve chute and it streamed out but did not open either. We plummeted directly down to the ground, where we crashed into the earth with a terrifying impact. I saw that without a doubt we were both killed. Covered with sweat, my heart pounding, and my mouth dry as cotton, I opened my eyes and gulped air. I felt that I had just received a clear warning not to make the jump. I saw that Carlos needed me and that I should not take risks with my life when I had an obligation to be a father to him.

I realized in that moment that I would have to cancel the jump. I agonized over what I would say to Jan and how I would justify offering a course about overcoming fear if I cancelled. The next day I called Jan but, unable to reach her, I left a message saying I would not be going with her this time. I did not hear back from her.

Two days later on the day of the jump, I was outdoors working in the yard when my daughter, Anna, came out of the house with a look on her face I will never forget. White as a sheet, she said, "Dad, it's Jan. She's dead."

In a state of shock I could hardly believe what I had heard. "What!" I babbled.

Anna struggled on. "Her chute didn't open. She died with a student."

I staggered into the house to find Lena on the phone getting further details. Jan had been tandem jumping with a series of students. In a tandem jump, the instructor pushes the student out the door of the plane as the student jumps. All the jumps had gone well until her chute failed to open and the rare event happened: the reserve chute failed to open and they both fell to their deaths. The crater they made was fifteen feet around and two feet deep. Nothing was left of their bodies.

My shock and tears lasted a long time. In fact, the event took me many months to get over, and to this day it marks a turning point in my life. Even now the thought of it brings tears to my eyes.

I had many considerations about the accident. If I had not cancelled, would the other student have lived? If I had not cancelled, would there have been a chance that Jan and I would have survived the jump? Was I meant to die this way? Had I just put off the inevitable? In an event of this magnitude it is difficult to maneuver alone through the emotion and confusion; I definitely needed support. I consulted my wisest friends and colleagues. They were considerate and extremely helpful to me, and I will always be grateful to them.

What I gleaned from this event was the following: I had an exit point that I might have taken. I chose not to. Instead, a person who had chosen to leave stepped in and took my place. In retrospect it was clear that there were various reasons for Jan to leave at this time. When I chose not to go with her, she simply went with another. Those who spoke to her just prior to her accident revealed that she seemed to know that she was going to die. She seemed happier than she had been in a long time. She even said to one friend the morning of the jump, "If I don't come back, just know I was doing what I love the most." She knew.

Later I thought of the warning Ananda had given me—"A woman will push you"—and I shivered. Obviously there are choices and I had made mine: to not jump, to father my son, to remain faithful in my relationship with Lena, and to live longer to make a larger contribution. A possibility, a probability was bypassed in favor of other options and I am glad of that choice.

A couple of weeks following the accident, I went to the Santa Fe ski basin after a big snowfall. Jan and I had skied there together shortly before her death. She had taken a bad fall on that day, which had rattled my nerves, and we had become separated once, leaving me feeling panicky until she at last reappeared, laughing, "Where were you, slowpoke?"

Now the experience of skiing there was bittersweet—I couldn't get Jan off my mind. The day was magnificent, and the conditions couldn't have been better. The slopes were covered with new cottony white billows of dry powder snow. In the afternoon I was skiing rapidly down an open slope high on the mountain near where Jan had fallen weeks before. Suddenly, such a powerful wind blasted up the mountain that I was almost stopped in my tracks. I had to throw my arms out like wings to keep my balance. From that location a grand vista of the Rio Grande Valley spread out below me. Then I distinctly heard Jan's laughing voice say to me, "This is what it's like to fly, José." She seemed so happy and carefree that I laughed out loud. After that, I relaxed and no longer felt mournful for the rest of the day. I knew Jan was okay and had chosen correctly for herself.

POSTSCRIPT

You will find that death plays a major role in many of the stories in this book. This is because death is such an amazing teacher and is always an encounter with major power. Rather than be afraid of death, it is beneficial to experience it as our friend. Without it there can be no birth, no renewal, no evolution in our approach to life. Death is also an illusion, like everything that is impermanent. Death is a tool that teaches. Nothing more. One day we will look and see that death never really existed.

So where is the power in this story? It brings up the question of free will versus fate, freedom of choice versus being entrapped in a preordained program. If everything is predestined, where is the power? If life is an already written movie, why bother? So does choice have to do with selecting a different path, or does choice only have to do with choosing what was already destined as opposed to resisting it? What I have learned is that it is not an either-or question, nor is the choice between resignation and acceptance. Both are deeply intertwined. The power is in choosing. If we fight what is handed to us, it goes badly for us. If we choose to accept our lessons, we build power and some-times we open a portal to a new choice.

What is the difference between resignation and acceptance? Acceptance gives us wiggle room and resignation does not.

There is a plan to life and there is ample wiggle room to shift probabilities if we learn certain lessons. In the end it looks to our minds as if each set of probabilities was destined no matter which set we chose. Some things just aren't completely understandable. What is clear is that I was in a powerful place at a powerful time in my life, meeting with powerful people discussing powerful topics—and powerful things happened.

EXERCISES

Reflect back over some of the major events of your life. What if the outcome had been different? Where would that outcome have led you? If that had been your reality, would you have experienced it as inevitable? Would you have accepted it the way it turned out?

¤

Imagine that you could project yourself a thousand years ahead of today and look back on your experiences. Are you glad for what happened? Are you accepting of the experiences, seeing them as necessary steps in a long series of adventures? Would you change anything?

¤

Reflect upon what you believe about the inevitability of your future. What have you resigned yourself to—that you will always be bad at languages, not remember names, find math difficult? Are those your only alternatives? Are there other outcomes awaiting you that lead to a different future?

¤

QUESTIONS

What should you accept as "just the way it is" and what should you question and choose to change? Consider your options. Are you actually free to choose or are you predestined?

2

THE RIGHT WAY
TO DIE

Clearly, my mother was as excited to see me as I was to see her, so I knew I had made the right decision to fly out to Northern California on Christmas Eve, 2005, when I got the call. She was slipping. For a ninety-nine-year-old woman suffering the discomforts of terminal spinal cancer, she had a great deal to express. I took notes and made recordings each day and evening I spent with her. Here is what we talked about.

¤

Margarita: "Yes, I'm so ready. I want to go soon. I'm tired. It's enough already. They are all waiting for me. Your dad, my friends, my mother, my father, my brothers. I want to see them. You are such a good son. I love you and I am very proud of you. I am finished with everything. There is nothing more to do. I'm just trouble now."

José: "Mom, you have a right to be trouble. You've taken care of so many people—your mother, your brothers, Dad, my brother and me, so many people. Now you're giving people a chance to take care of you. Maybe you won't go until you have experienced that for a little bit."

Margarita: "You think so? Well, that is an interesting way you put it. I guess you are right. But I'm really ready. The Lord needs to know that enough is enough. So, you think it will be soon?"

José: "Don't be too impatient, Mom. Dying takes time. It's a process that you have to go through. Yes, you are almost done here. I don't think it will be long, but you know it is a mystery and no one knows for sure when you will pass over."

Margarita: "Oh boy!" She sounded both excited and a little taken aback. Then she drifted off into a morphine-induced sleep.

✡

My mother, Margarita Saenz España Stevens, was born in 1907 in Guadalajara, Mexico, to a well-to-do family of Spanish-Basque heritage. Her father was district attorney in that city before the Mexican Revolution. His marriage to my grandmother was arranged between two wealthy families. She was given to him at age eleven when he was already thirty. At first, she only wanted to play with dolls. Then came seven sons and two daughters. Margarita was the third child. The next girl died and then came three more boys, but one of these, José, died in childhood. Being the only girl in a Mexican family was not an easy task: four brothers to guard your every move and all the women's work handed to you. When the Mexican Revolution came in 1910, all hell broke loose. The revolutionary war lasted for ten years until she was thirteen.

✡

Margarita, speaking haltingly: "Revolution and war is a horrible thing. Don't let anyone romanticize war. It is one of the worst things a human being can experience. We barely survived and many didn't."

José: "You've seen a lot. That is a hard thing to have to experience when you are so young. You are a real veteran of life."

Margarita: "The city alternated between federal forces and rebel forces with fierce battles being waged on the streets for control of the city. I was made to lie on the floor as the bullets flew through the glass windows. I remember soldiers crawling like snakes up the street with their weapons. After the shooting stopped, the street was littered with dead bodies. Anything that moved died, including lots of civilians.

"When the rebels under Carranza and Villa wrested control of the city from the federals, they seized my father, your grandfather, and arrested him. Although he fought hard and at great sacrifice for the rights of indigenous peoples against the land grabs of the federals, he was still a court-appointed official and thus on the wrong side."

Tearfully now: "I went to see my father in prison. He didn't want me to see him there but I just had to go. It was a terrible place, freezing, with green moss on the walls. There were thousands of people crowded into the cells. He was such a good man and didn't deserve to be there. More than anything I wanted him to come home. When he did, it was too late. A year in a Mexican prison is a horrific experience and although my mother fought to free him, displaying extraordinary courage by facing down the rebel generals, by the time she succeeded he was a broken man. At age twelve I nursed him for six months, but his health was destroyed and he died of infection and pneumonia, leaving our family to fend for itself."

José: "You are no stranger to death. But you've outlived everyone."

Margarita: "Oooooohhhh! I've seen so many people die. You don't know how precious life is until you know what death is. My mother, Maria, your nana, was extremely tough and began to do cooking and catering to support the family. Three of the boys, your uncles, went to work, but one, age twelve, was kidnapped by the rebels and sent to fight with them against the federals. He was only twelve at the time but my mother succeeded in tracking him down and bringing him home. So tough was my mother that one day bandits broke into the house and she singlehandedly ordered them out with a broom. They backed out rather than deal with her."

◻

After her father died, Margarita took over managing the household. She took over her eldest brother's care when he came down with tuberculosis even while struggling to overcome severe asthma herself. For seven years she nursed him until his death, all the while watching over a mother and another brother slowly succumbing to alcoholism. Tough as she was, my grandmother began to abuse the bottle.

The family moved to the frontier, the Imperial Valley, where there was an abundance of jobs for young engineers and city planners and dry air for Margarita's asthma. While all her brothers went to Jesuit schools, Margarita was expected to take care of everyone else and never went beyond the fifth grade. Yet she clearly demonstrated signs of great artistic talent, painting portraits with oils whenever she could. She took trips to San Diego during the summers that were simply too hot in Mexicali. There, she did touch-up work for photographers and advertisers. When she was in her thirties, she asserted her independence by going to Los Angeles, getting her green card, and obtaining a position as an illustrator at the *Los Angeles Times*. It was an excellent job and she carried it until she met my dad, an American of English-Irish descent in his late forties. He had been a confirmed bachelor but within three months they were married, and soon they started a family at my mother's comparatively late age of thirty-nine.

There followed years of childrearing, two boys to be exact, while my mother worked with my father in his stage lighting business. They became known as lighting experts in the tough Hollywood film and theater industries, but the work was hard—and not only decidedly unglamorous, but hazardous. There were high voltages, leaded black paint, high concentrations of asbestos, and mercury. I know about these things because I grew up working for my parents.

◻

Three days later . . .

Margarita, somewhat annoyed: "So! I'm still here and I haven't had any dreams. Nothing. And I haven't seen an angel yet. My hands and feet are still warm. I don't know . . . sometimes I have my doubts."

José: "That's normal, Mom. Everybody has doubts at times. You are being impatient. You will see. All these things will happen in good time. This process might take a week."

Margarita: "A week! Oh, no." A dejected look.

José: "The angel might look like a bright light."

Margarita: "I want an angel with wings."

José, smiling: "What color wings?"

Margarita: "Pink! Pink wings."

José: "Like a flamingo."

Margarita, laughing: "Yes. There is enough room in here for him. And I'm glad I have this nice big window because he can come flying right in. Do you think the trees will get in the way?"

José: "The angel might just appear in here. Doesn't have to fly in like Superman. I don't see the trees as a problem." Amused, Margarita smiles and drifts off to sleep again.

In addition to supporting and caring for my grandmother, Margarita always found ways to help local people, whether it was a new immigrant family, a single mother, an elderly couple, or a poor family. This earned her much respect and friendship, especially in the Hispanic community. Through the eyes of a young child like me who wanted her all to myself, it seemed like she was always working, always helping out other people, and I resented that immensely, especially when she went through her grumpy years of menopause.

Adolescence found me out of the house every chance I could get. Basically from age seventeen on, I headed out and returned home only for brief visits. I needed to get away from Mom's artisan chaos, her unpredictable moods, and the constant efforts to mold me or reinvent me according to Catholic doctrine. I went to Northern California and lived my own life for a long time, and only after many years did I discover that my mother had been hiding something from me: the extent of my father's gradual deterioration from Alzheimer's. I had chalked his behavior up to forgetfulness and Mom's overblown worries, but I finally saw the real picture. Mom was trying to take care of someone who needed way more help than she could give.

My brother and I arranged for him to be taken to a nursing home in Northern California, and Mom moved into a retirement community next door. She was eighty-two and had already outlived three of her brothers.

My relationship with her seemed to revive then. I had moved with my family to New Mexico but visited as often as I could. Nine months later, as Mom and I held his hands, Dad died, leaving Mom with a big hole to fill. As he took his last breath, she looked at me with the most accepting and serene face I have ever seen and said simply, "He's gone." Lightning flashed outside, and the heavens opened up with a fierce deluge of rain. I was overcome with awe—I had never known that death could be so powerful.

I told my mother, "When it's your time, I want to be there for you too."

She said, "I would like that."

After that I worried about Mom, but I needn't have bothered. I was amazed and inspired to see her transformation at that late age. She went out and got art supplies and began to paint with oils and acrylics on canvases large and small. She even had an art exposition at the local community art center where people fought over her paintings. She transferred all the energy it had taken to care for Dad and soon became like an angel of mercy to the community in and outside of her retirement community.

She got to know the mostly Mexican staff and counseled their families about all kinds of problems. She read to people, helped people younger than she was walk to the dining area, and went out of her way to befriend the few Spanish speakers who were somewhat isolated. Over the next fourteen years she outlived scores of people by walking a mile every day and being of service to everyone. She was an exceptionally popular figure and people always wanted her company. When elderly men tried to court her, she simply said she was a one-man woman and wasn't interested. Finally, when her eyes went and her hands shook too badly, she put her brushes away. I knew then that this was the beginning of the end of her stay on earth.

Margarita: "I look like a scarecrow. I could scare the birds if they saw me now."

José: "Mom, there you go again. You look fine. You are a wonderful being besides. It doesn't matter how you look. Remember when you used to take care of birds as a kid? You put splints on their broken feet and fixed their wings."

Margarita: "Yeah, I couldn't have dogs or cats because I had asthma so bad. But later when we had dogs, they would do everything I told them. They used to help me with your dad. I would tell them to watch him and if he was going to get into some kind of trouble to come and get me. The dogs would come and grab my sleeve and pull me when they wanted me to come. They were good dogs, those two. Life is so mysterious."

José: "Yeah, it is, but soon you are going to find out all the answers to your questions. I am very excited for you. You are going on a great adventure."

Margarita: "Adventure. You are the adventurous one. Well, if I find out anything, I will tell you. You think I can do that, with telepathy?"

José: "Sure, that will be easy for you. I would love it if you could answer some questions for me. You could visit me in dreams and give me information about what you find out."

Margarita: "Can people really do that?"

José: "Yes, they can, if they want. You don't have to, though. It's up to you."

Margarita: "You are full of stories. You have traveled so much. You are a smart guy, but me, I don't know anything."

José: "Where do you think I learned to tell stories? I grew up on your stories about Mexico. Dad told stories too. You were great storytellers. I got my sense of adventure from both of you. You know, wisdom is different from education. You didn't get a formal education but you have become a very wise person from just living life."

Margarita: "That's what your dad used to say. He said I was very smart. But I'm not wise. I don't know anything. The Lord has helped me very much."

José: "See? That's what I mean. You are wise enough to know that you don't know anything. It's the really dumb ones who think they know it all."

Margarita, laughing: "I'm glad you're here. You are a lot of fun and a good son. I'm very happy."

José: "Want to hear some stories?"

Margarita: "Sure."

I tell her stories about Guadalupe, my Huichol teacher from Mexico, and his philosophy of life. I tell her about magic healings and include tales about the Shipibo people from the Amazon, what they believe about life and death, and how they sing *icaros* (sacred songs) to heal each other. I tell her about shamans and medicine people. Then I have her listen to a tape of icaros from the Amazon. She is delighted.

◻

Mom was always a devoted Catholic. For much of her life she believed in all the Catholic doctrine—heaven and hell, paying for sins, good people and bad people, and so on. We had many arguments over the criminal behavior of the church and its blatant hypocrisy, but her Catholicism was emotional and had little to do with ideas. She was also very conservative politically because my father was. We used to have huge intellectual debates about politics, and I would get so upset about what seemed to be her complete refusal to look at the facts. I couldn't understand how she could believe in an administration that gave to the rich and deprived her of social services that she needed so badly. It wasn't until later that I saw that her beliefs were tied to my father and his memory. Then it didn't matter anymore.

◻

Several days later . . .

Margarita, whispering now: "It's a huge thing what you have done for me. You came all the way from New Mexico when I needed you. Thank you so. I love you dearly."

José, tearfully: "I wouldn't have it any other way. It's an honor for me to be here with you in your transition. You have done so much for me. You carried me around for nine months and made it possible for me to grow up. You gave me a good education, the foundation for my good fortune. Thank you. I love you."

Margarita: "You did that yourself. You took advantage of what we gave you. It was the Lord who helped me. I didn't do anything."

José: "Mom, there is one thing you need to do before you go. You need to see clearly what a wonderful person you are. That is very, very important if you are going to make a successful transition."

Margarita: "But I'm not a wonderful person."

José: "Well, God made you, didn't he? And God only makes wonderful things, right?"

Margarita, reluctantly, seeing where this was going: "Yeeessss . . . "

José: "So that makes you wonderful, doesn't it?

Margarita: "Well, if you say so."

José, thinking: *$@&*! She didn't let that in, as usual.*

Margarita: "Well, thank you. I never saw it that way before."

José, with relief: "You are a wonderful person. You've helped so many people and taken care of them. You have an eye for beauty and color. You are a very unique personality, and there has never been and will never be someone just like you. You have done Margarita perfectly. Everyone I talk to respects you and loves you. You have no enemies, and no one thinks badly of you. You've worked very hard and made a contribution. The world is better because you have been here. I admire you, and I am inspired by you."

Margarita: "How do you know all of that?"

José: "I'm just telling you what I have heard and seen for myself. It seems to be so."

Margarita, drifting off to sleep: "I'm very happy."

An hour later . . .

Margarita: "Someone was here while you were out of the room. They fixed my covers."

José: "I was standing right outside. I didn't see anyone go in."

Margarita: "Well, it was someone because they adjusted the covers around my chest and neck."

José: "I guess you had a visitor from the other side."

Margarita: "Hmmm."

The next day . . .

I arrive early and outside her door offer some tobacco to Spirit for a painless transition, as I do every morning. I light her candle and burn a little Palo Santo from Peru to clear the air in her room. Then, using feathers, I ask that all negativity and fears be removed from Mom so that she is light and free to go. Lastly I anoint her with Agua Florida (perfumed water) and some frankincense from a small bottle, concentrating on asking for wisdom, love, and power to move into her heart. I rearrange the Shipibo cloth on her bed. It is covered with designs for clear visions.

Margarita, much weaker: "How long do you think it's going to be? What if it's another week?"

José: "You're almost ready. Spirit must have a few things more for you to experience because you are still here. You can't hurry it up. It will take as long as it takes."

Margarita: "Hmmph."

That evening . . .

Margarita, whispering: "Cathy and Frank came by tonight while you were at dinner. I'm worried about Cathy. She doesn't seem happy. All she did was complain. I felt so depressed when she left. I wanted to talk to Frank but she monopolized the conversation just talking about herself. My heart is racing. I can't seem to calm down."

José, really annoyed: "That's not right. This is your special time. You shouldn't have to worry about anyone else at this time. That is so inappropriate and selfish. You have such little time left and it is precious. I'm going to talk to her and Frank."

Margarita: "No. Don't say anything. I don't want trouble."

José: "Trouble? I won't stand for any more of this. Don't worry! I'll be diplomatic. But she needs to know that from now on she can't use you as a sounding board. What is the matter with her? Doesn't she get it? This is a time for you to say good-bye. As far as I'm concerned, this is a temple and what you are going through is too important. Don't worry about her. She has to solve her own problems. She is a distraction. You have more important things to do. Just put her out of your mind, and I'll make sure you get to talk to Frank alone."

Margarita: "Thank you."

¤

I was so agitated that I had a great deal of trouble calming down. I realized that Mom always put up with way too much. She couldn't say no to younger souls who behaved like children. When I was a kid she knew a lot about setting limits, but in her later years that seemed to fall away. This was the martyrdom side of the impatience she struggled with.

Margarita: "Salvador [her long-dead favorite brother] just offered me a cookie."

José: "That is so nice. He's helping you from the other side."

Margarita: "Yes, there are others too. This is so wonderful, to have all this love and help. God is so good. I don't know what I would have done without you helping me. The Lord arranged this. I am so lucky." Tears.

✡

Later . . .

Margarita: "Somebody is opening a door. I can't quite see them. There is someone there."

José: "Sounds like they are opening the door for you now so you can go through soon. The other side is helping."

Margarita: "Wonderful."

✡

Later, after a number of visitors . . .

Margarita: "Will it be very long now?"

José: "Not long. But maybe there is a little more for you to do."

Margarita: "Oh, what could I do anymore that is useful?"

José: "You know, Mom, I am noticing how moved everyone is when they come to visit you. It's as if you are in a state of grace and people benefit from just being with you. They go away healed. You don't have to do anything. I sense the presence of helpers and great beings around you helping you. All your helpers from the other side are here. I think others feel that too. That is very powerful. You are acting as a messenger and perhaps that is a last contribution."

Margarita, eyes filled with tears: "Ohhhh. You think so. I can tell you are not kidding. You are serious. That is so wonderful. God is so good. There is so much love in the world. Dear God, forgive me for anything I have done wrong. Forgive everyone.

I love you. Guide me and bless my family. Bless my son, José. He is a good son. He is helping me."

José: Can't speak—very moved.

▢

Later . . .

Margarita: "Where is Frank? I haven't talked to Frank. God says I can't go yet, not until I talk to Frank."

José: "He came the other day, Mom. He's coming again tonight. He couldn't come yesterday so he's coming today."

I sneak out of the room and call him on the phone, leaving him a message. "Mom's asking for you. She's slipping away. Better come if you want to see her."

▢

Later that evening after her visit with Frank. I return from dinner . . .

Margarita, struggling with the *bardos* (transitional states): "Oh! There are devils. They keep trying to get me. I try to get rid of them but they keep coming back. I called the police. They are coming to get rid of them. Oh, I'm so confused. I think I'm going nuts. What's the matter with me? Is there grain all over the floor?"

José: "No grain. What you are feeling is part of the process, Mom. The Tibetans call them the bardos. They are challenges you must face. The devils are really your own fears that are confronting you. You are being tested. You must not resist them or give them any energy. They exist only in your mind. If you struggle with them, you are feeding them. It sounds like the visit with Frank was difficult. What happened?"

Margarita: "So you mean the devil wasn't here earlier trying to ruin things in the family? Frank told me I didn't love him. I told him I loved him but he didn't believe me. I think he is angry I'm not leaving any money. I thought the devil was here trying to interfere."

José: "There isn't any actual devil, Mom. The devil is a human creation. God is everywhere and created everything. How can there be a devil?"

Margarita: "Oh. I am so glad to hear that. But Frank—he thinks I don't love him. What can I do? Maybe I can tell his wife and she will tell him. Do you think that is a good idea?"

José: "No. I don't think so, Mom. That will not help. I'm not sure who said what in your conversation. I'm sorry you're upset. I don't think he expects any money from you. He knows the situation. Dying brings up a lot of old feelings in people. But just remember, the devil is a creation of our own fears. You are thinking too much. Just make it simple. There is only being loved and loving others to the best of your ability. I think you have done the best you could. This is not a perfect world, so you can't necessarily fix other people's feelings. But you can adjust your own. Here, let me play you some music."

I put some earphones on her head and play her beautiful music.

Margarita: Relieved. Calms down.

José: Pensive. Exhausted. Thinking, *Some parts of dying are really hard!*

◻

The next day . . .

Margarita, eyes closed and greatly agitated: "There are water faucets open and water is running all over the floor!"

José: "That is not a problem, Mom. Everything is okay. Don't get distracted with fears now. Remember what I told you."

Margarita, with relief: "Oh, it's okay. I'm glad you are here." She spends most of the day sleeping.

◻

The next day . . .

Now her eyes are closed almost continuously. She speaks very slowly and so low that I can hardly understand her. She struggles to make the sign of the cross.

José: "Mom, I am going to have to go tomorrow. If you want to pass while I am here, I will be here until two o'clock tomorrow afternoon. Then I have to return to Santa Fe to get an MRI on my knee that has been scheduled for a long time. If you are still not ready to go and need more time, Shirley [her good friend] will be here with you. It's whatever you need to do."

Margarita, with a peaceful smile, successfully making the sign of the cross over me: "Okay. You take care of yourself."

◻

We had no other verbal contact, and as far as I know that is the last thing my mother ever said. She died peacefully at dawn about thirty-six hours later. No one was present in the room with her—a good thing. That way she could pass without distraction.

There is great power in encountering death, especially that of a parent. It was perhaps one of the most powerful events of my life. I learned so much, felt so much, put so much together. In some ways I truly matured as a man in the process. I can only hope I show up for my own death as my mom did for hers. During those few days I spent with her, I felt fully validated by her for the first time ever. Prior to that I never measured up in her eyes because she thought I was a fallen-away Catholic. But during those days what I was no longer mattered; she saw me, and I saw her without all the doctrine. The result was many blessings. I never tire of telling this story, the story of her passing and my witnessing it.

POSTSCRIPT

There is no question that confronting our own or another's death is one of the most powerful experiences we can have. Death, of course, involves mystery and therein lies the power. Death is also a transition, an edge between one existence and another, the world of dreams, *maya*, and suffering on the one hand and the world of truth, love, and pure essence on the other. Edges always hold power, shamanically speaking: the edge between night and day, between one season and another, and between sleep and waking. These edges bear much fruit and bring us our strongest creative visions. That is why they are honored wherever people walk the shamanic path.

Although this experience was about death, in my mind it was also about life. Those few days I spent with my mother were the most life-affirming days I ever spent with her. It was worth a lifetime of ordinary visits with her. Therefore, death and life cannot be separated. Every day some death is happening within us, and every day more life is given birth. What a grand mystery!

EXERCISES

Look in the mirror and know that when it is time, this body will eventually die. Write your own obituary from the point of view that you were a tragic figure, perhaps coming to an untimely end. Life was stacked against you and you finally lost the battle. Write another obituary with you as the hero or heroine completing a grand, productive adventure and dying with glory. Does either one fit? Perhaps there is a third obituary that is more accurate than these two. How would you express your transition artistically?

3

LOST IN MEXICO

Seven years after our Huichol teacher, Guadalupe, died, I was once again traveling to Wirikuta, the sacred peyote fields in central Mexico, on our annual pilgrimage. This time I was traveling with Lena; my daughter, Anna; and Anna's relatively new boyfriend, Aaron (who is now her husband). We were crammed into Anna's Subaru Forester for the thirteen-hundred-mile journey from New Mexico.

We left Santa Fe early in the morning and stopped at the *aduana*, the place about fifty kilometers past the border where travelers register their cars and get permits. Lena discovered that she had brought her recently expired passport instead of her new one and would not be able to continue. Shocked, we all had to instantly reorganize—this complication didn't change the fact that we still needed to join with our group to the south as planned to conduct the ceremony. We drove Lena back to the edge of Juarez, where she grabbed a taxi for the border to explore her options for meeting up with us again. Meanwhile, Anna, Aaron, and I headed down to Mexico. Knowing how resourceful Lena is, I was not worried about her.

Two days later we were in Wadley, a tiny pueblo deep in Mexico, waiting to meet our group. Suddenly they arrived in two cars and, of course, Lena was with them. She had experienced many adventures, including a taxi that broke down and another taxi that ran out of gas, but she had gone to El Paso, gotten our assistant to overnight-mail the passport, headed back to Juarez, and caught a flight to Monterrey just in time to be picked up by members of our group.

We had a fabulous pilgrimage with an overnight ceremony in the desert, Aaron's first outside the Native American Church he had grown up in. The ceremony was an adjustment for him after his experience with Arapaho-style ceremonies, which were always very formal and followed a strict protocol. Huichol ceremonies are by contrast loosely conducted, with time allowed for singing, storytelling, and socializing. Interestingly, some traditional lore has it that the North American indigenous nations were taught by the Huichol centuries ago but that their ceremonies became formalized and rule-oriented because of their masculine orientation. The Huichol are more feminine in orientation.

In the morning we made our climb up Cerro Quemado, the sacred mountain, and then, as always, we retraced our thirteen hundred miles back to Santa Fe. On the second day of driving, Aaron was at the wheel and I was dozing on and off in the backseat, deep into my book, when the car sputtered a few times and we came to a standstill by the side of the highway in the Sonoran Desert, sand dunes in the distance. We had run out of gas. Aaron had been enjoying the scenery so much that he had not noticed when the reserve light came on. Since I spoke some Spanish it was determined I should go get the gas—and quickly. Within five minutes I was standing on the other side of the highway hitchhiking back to the last town, maybe twenty miles back. Being in a pilgrimage frame of mind, I asked for help from Spirit and contemplated that I was about to enter a mysterious journey with unknown consequences.

Within minutes a Mexican salesman stopped and picked me up. Evidently very successful, he was driving a late-model car and speeding up to a hundred miles per hour. After a pleasant conversation, he dropped me off at the gas station unexpectedly quickly, where I met a nice woman attendant who got some Clorox bottles and filled them up with gas. She asked a waiting truck driver if he would give me a lift, and within minutes I was headed back up the highway in a truck loaded with Volvo parts. I thought, *They'll be surprised at how quickly I got the gas and came back.* I was feeling good. Everything was going like clockwork until we arrived at the exact spot and kilometer mark sign where I had left the car. Lo and behold, the car had vanished along with all my family.

I had to think rapidly about what to do with this turn of events. The truck driver did not want to leave me stranded in the middle of the desert with the gas, and he suggested that a car must have stopped and given them gas and that they had probably gone on to the next gas station, where he could take me to meet them. He said that standing by the side of the road alone in the desert to wait for them was quite unsafe; having few good other choices, I reluctantly agreed.

We drove many miles and eventually arrived at the next gas station—which, as it happened, was boarded up and out of business. With a sinking feeling I realized I was now on a major unplanned adventure and I had a choice: to freak out or stay calm and enjoy the ride. I caught myself starting to feel sorry for myself but remembered Guadalupe's admonition to me years before at a campfire in Wirikuta. No, I could not afford that indulgence. I was on a major initiation here, a test of my abilities to manage this situation. I had to man up and meet the challenge with humor and initiative.

The truck drove on northward toward the border, and eventually the road forked into a toll road and a free road. The truck took the free route, so now I knew there was even less possibility of meeting up with my crew, considering that none of our cell phones worked in Mexico. Eventually we got to the original aduana where Lena had been forced to turn back, and I chuckled grimly about how this adventure was like bookends: first Lena and now me with a sudden change of plans. Somehow we could not manage to keep four people in the car at once during this trip. I thanked the truck driver, gave him the gas, and got out to wait for the others, hoping they would come this way and hoping I was ahead of them. It was time to call in my allies, which I did big time.

The sun was going down, the wind had started to blow, and I was wearing nothing but a T-shirt, shorts, and sandals. I had no food, water, or anything but my wallet and, thank God, my passport. I checked my wallet and found a twenty-dollar bill inside. Better twenty than nothing. Still, things looked grim—I would have to become very creative. I waited for about an hour and a half before deciding I had better try to get home on my own. It was now dark. I walked to a gas station and bought some water and happened to look in a mirror. I hadn't shaved in four or five days, my eyes were bloodshot, my hair was windblown and wild, and my scant clothes were dirty. I had that disheveled look that people get after an all-night peyote ceremony. In appearance I was now becoming persona non grata. It is amazing how fast we slip down the social scale when unforeseen events occur.

I asked some locals if there were any buses or taxis into Juarez and was told there were none. I would have to hitch a ride. There were long lines of cars returning their car permits, so I walked up and down making inquiries and receiving nothing but rejection: people rolled up their windows when they saw me coming. Even the Mexicans didn't like the way I looked, a guy in shorts with no luggage and a wild look approaching them at night.

Finally, as I was about to despair, a Mexican couple with an infant offered me a ride and I was on the road again. Perhaps they were angels or my helping spirits taking form and helping me out. I don't know. More conventionally, I figured we had some agreement or they were creating some nice positive karma with me, and I was most grateful. Just into Juarez they turned off the road, so I thanked them and got out into the dangerous, sketchy Juarez night, a place known as the death capital of Mexico, one of the most treacherous cities in the world.

Fortunately, there was a run-down taxi nearby that I hailed and asked to take me to the border. The driver said okay but after two blocks the car broke down and I had to get out. I hailed another wreck of a taxi and, sputtering and crabbing down the road, we got to the border. I walked into El Paso using my passport and bought a nylon ghetto jacket for ten bucks and a bus ticket to Santa Fe on Americanos, the laborers' express. I found an ancient pay phone and called the only number I knew by heart—home. I left a message: "In El Paso . . . headed home . . . will take bus . . . arrive 1 A.M. at Giant gas station . . . hope you are all okay . . . I am fine."

I thought maybe Lena and crew would have contacted Sarah, our assistant, at her home. Sarah could retrieve messages off our home phone and relay my message to them. It seemed like a long shot, but what else could I do? I had just enough money left to buy a snack and, for a dollar, a terrible pillow filled with crunchy foam squares for the ride home.

The battered Americanos bus finally arrived and, pulling out my ticket, a thin slip of paper, I waited in line to get on. Next thing I knew, the wind was gusting and blowing up a lot of dust and suddenly my slip of paper tore from my fingers and blew under the bus. I ran to retrieve it but could not find it in the dark. I ran around to the other side of the bus, but the ticket was gone. I did not have enough money for another ticket, and I was horrified at my predicament. By the time I got back around to the door of the bus, everyone had loaded in and it was ready to go. I went up the steps and told the bus driver in my best Spanish what had happened, that I had bought a legitimate ticket but that it had blown away and become lost. He looked at me like I was a complete con artist. Desperate and thinking fast, I told him that the woman at the window selling tickets could vouch for me and I asked him if he would just be willing to ask her if I had bought a ticket for Santa Fe from her. I was in luck because Mexicans are used to these kinds of unlikely predicaments. He went with me to the window and indeed the woman there told him I had bought a ticket for Santa Fe a couple of hours earlier. I was in business again. He let me on the bus, the only American on board.

All the other passengers were Mexican laborers headed for points north. They all looked at me with pity: poor American guy down on his luck. I fell sound asleep on my wonderful, terrible, crunchy pillow, and when I awoke I looked out the window to see snow blowing in the glow of the headlights. A few hours later I was in Santa Fe with the snow still falling.

I was wondering what I would do if my family was not there to pick me up. I would have to walk home in the snow—a distance of about ten miles—in my shorts and sandals. Maybe I could find a taxi. I got off the bus and—guess what? There was my family waiting for me, with many apologies and much relief. I told them no apologies were needed, that I'd had quite the unexpected adventure but was fine. Yes, they had gotten my message. Yes, they had gotten gas from a passing stranger five minutes after I left. They thought they could catch me, but the salesman drove so fast that they never could. They spent hours in the desert driving back and forth trying to find me, finally giving up and figuring I was on my own and would make it back. When they got to the border and received the message that I was arriving by bus at 1 A.M., they drove a hundred miles an hour to get there on time. Lena—being movement-centered and liking to speed—drove that portion.

Aaron, not surprisingly, was terrified. He figured he had just singlehandedly lost his future father-in-law in Mexico and that his entire relationship with Anna was in jeopardy. He was convinced I would chew him out royally for running out of gas, but I was never angry with him. I knew I was under some kind of Pluto Saturn transit and had actually gotten off easy. I only felt badly that everyone was so worried for so long. Aaron and the rest of my family were just the actors in my adventure drama, and they played their parts perfectly. I was simply happy to see them, my heart open, full of thanks and forgiveness for whatever had taken place. Best of all, I knew this would make an excellent story. The best stories, of course, are the misadventures where catastrophe rears its head but in the end all is well.

POSTSCRIPT

I had time to have many feelings and thoughts during this adventure. Mainly I realized how amazingly out of control life can seem at times and how it can test us to the limit when we are least expecting it. Reacting with fear or anger is worse than useless because it promotes a negative outcome. The only solution is to be proactive by enjoying the event and making sure that the outcome is resonant with positive feelings and thoughts.

Sudden spontaneous events are filled with power. Remember that they involve a mystery, a place where power likes to reside. They inhabit the border between the predictable world of known events and those unknown to the personality. The trick is to realize in the moment that the personality seldom knows what is happening and that this is perfectly fine because essence knows exactly how to navigate. This requires something called trust: trust in Spirit and trust in self, trust that all will be well. The initiation is not designed to defeat but to teach about becoming powerful.

EXERCISE

Reflect on times when you have been lost—physically, emotionally, and/or psychologically. How did you lose your way? How did you approach your dilemma? How did you go about getting found? In hindsight, were you really lost or just in transition? Were there antagonists or was it you, your worst enemy, who gave you the most trouble? How would you tell this in story form?

4

THE GUATEMALA TEST
AND INITIATION

ometimes, even when we're doing everything right, essence
throws curves at us just to see how we will manage them. This
is the tale of such a test and perhaps an example of one way of
managing it, along with lessons learned.

After an extraordinary trip to the Huayllay Stone Forest in
the Andes of central Peru, Anna and I stopped in Guatemala
to do some pre-planning before taking our two-year program
group there to work with Mayan shamans. In Peru our group
had worked with the Q'ero, the powerful Andean *paqos*, or shamans, who had been teaching us. After a series of wonderful
ceremonies at fourteen thousand to fifteen thousand feet, we
felt strong and filled with light. Our hearts were open and our
sense of connection to Spirit was strong. So Anna and I figured
we would bring this good foundation with us on our research
trip to Guatemala.

Guatemala was all mist and clouds, with occasional moments
of hot tropical sun. We would map out a Mayan adventure; meet
with shamans; plan ceremonies, transportation, hotels, and

itinerary; and organize general logistics for a group of twenty. We headed deep into the Mayan land of mystery, Lake Atitlán, a true place of great power. After scoping out surrounding towns, markets, and ceremonial places, we were ready to head out for Tikal, the great Mayan ruins in the north, and then on to other adventures. We decided to take a day off and relax in Panajachel, a tourist-oriented town on the shores of Lake Atitlán with great views of the surrounding volcanoes. We found a nice hotel along the main street where we could relax . . . and that is where this adventure begins.

As we checked in, I noticed a woman who appeared to be a hotel guest sitting on a couch outside her room watching us. We entered our room, laid down our luggage, and since a strong rainstorm was taking place we settled in for a good nap. Earlier we had changed some money at the local bank, as we had more traveling to do and the banks would be closed the next day, Sunday. I stuffed a good amount into my wallet and gave the rest to Anna, who stowed it in her luggage and locked it up because there were no safe deposit boxes in this hotel.

After we awoke from our nap and the skies had cleared, we decided to go out and get a bite to eat and do some shopping in the colorful marketplace. As we were leaving and locking up the room, I noticed that, curiously, the same woman was still sitting on the couch watching us. The hotel seemed secure so I didn't think much of it, and we went out. We had a wonderful time that afternoon exploring, eating, bargaining, and finding great gifts in the marketplace. We even found a location to do some great prayers and connect in with the Spirit of that place.

About sunset we made our way back to the hotel and upon arriving found the door to our room not only unlocked but splintered. The room had been ransacked. Our belongings were scattered everywhere, the luggage lay open, the contents were disgorged, and we realized that the robbers had made off with all our reserve money,

Anna's reserve credit card, her driver's license, her expensive video camera, and my iPhone. At first it appeared her passport was gone too but we found it strangely safe under the bed. We guessed that in their haste the robbers must have pulled out the contents of the document case and the passport slid away out of sight. Since an American passport is worth about ten thousand dollars on the black market, obviously we were being watched over and protected from a worse fate.

As we witnessed this chaos, damage, and loss, I felt oddly neutral. I quickly assessed the loss; it appeared to be about twenty-five hundred dollars' worth. All items could be replaced and we were not hurt. Both passports were fine, as I had carried mine with me. Nevertheless, I summoned the clerk at the desk to witness the robbery scene—and this is where the greater part of the adventure began.

The clerk was horrified that this had happened on his watch and he said he would call the owner immediately as well as the police. In short order the owner arrived, a lean German man in his fifties who spoke good English. I shall call him Hans. He appeared distraught and kept saying what a bad thing this was, that it was impossible, that in twenty years of hotel ownership it had never happened and simply could not be. He asked what we had lost, and when we told him he was even more distraught and kept saying over and over that as the hotel owner it was his responsibility to make it right, to see to it that we were compensated. I was rather amazed at this since I did not really expect any compensation. Nevertheless, he said it was a matter of honor for him and that it was bad for business and the hotel's reputation.

Meanwhile, the police took forever to come. When they finally arrived they took many photos of the room and interviewed each of us. At first none of them or Hans knew we could speak Spanish so they thought we could not understand them. This led to some interesting aspects of the story. The police commented that we had probably left the room unlocked—then I pointed out a large screwdriver the thieves had used to break in. Meanwhile, Anna was busy on the hotel computer trying to cancel her credit card. As all this was going on, Hans's upper-class Guatemalan wife showed up carrying a Rottweiler puppy of just eight weeks. She instructed her husband that he must compensate us for all the losses, and she kept mentioning "mil dollares," a thousand dollars, as the sum he should pay us.

Now it turned out that the robbers had already tried to use the credit card eight times in just a few hours but failed each time except for buying a tank of gasoline. It was quickly established where the gas station was and someone was dispatched to interview the attendant, who said that the people using the credit card had commented about how cheap gas was in Guatemala and how much more expensive it was in El Salvador. Then someone noticed that the guests in room 6 had vanished but left their TV and lights on to make it seem like they were still there; the woman watching us as we checked in was one of the El Salvadoran robbers. It was a sophisticated inside job and they had scored.

By this time we were starving, having had no dinner, and it was getting late in the evening. Hans invited us to the restaurant next door, an establishment that he proudly said was the best place in town. Not wanting to take advantage of him, I ordered something modest and a beer, as did Anna. Hans waxed eloquent, saying he owned the entire hotel building and used to own the restaurant too. As we ate, he drank shots of tequila but did not eat. Meanwhile, the police had entered to enjoy a meal on his dime. We could see they all knew each other rather well, and there seemed to be some tension between them.

As Hans's tongue loosened with the drink, he began to swing rather oddly from one topic to another. He badly wanted us to know how successful he was, telling us that each fancy dinner plate in the restaurant he had brought personally from Germany and cost one hundred dollars apiece. At one point a couple entered the restaurant and he remarked to us that they were the richest people in Guatemala. He made a great display of going over to them and greeting them. Upon returning, he growled threateningly about how he was going to catch the thieves—and when he did he would kill them. I started to feel very uneasy. He went on to say that in Guatemala if you were caught for a crime like this the police would likely kill you before you even made it to jail, and if you went to jail the conditions were so bad you would not survive. He said he knew a hit man in El Salvador who could find and eliminate anyone. By this time he was quite drunk. He told us he had had an incident before but it was just a tourist trying to cash in on his insurance. He glared at us as if implying that we were trying to do the same thing.

I deduced that Hans was a young soul warrior who was caught between his desperate need to appear successful and wealthy and even magnanimous and his terrible reluctance to part with any of his money. He said things like, "Nobody f—s with Hans" while giving us hard stares. I realized at that point that somehow in his mind we had become the enemy and he was trying to intimidate us by threatening us so we wouldn't cause him any trouble. Then it came out that he was terrified of the police report we were about to file because it would cost him a lot of money; they would shut down his hotel for a month until all the paperwork was done. We could see that the police did not like him; in fact, they seemed to detest him, and it didn't seem far-fetched that they would stick it to him. He wanted us to come to some kind of agreement—we could write what we wanted in the report but he preferred we would say that the robbery had happened on a bus or somewhere else. I told him the police already knew it had happened at his hotel but he said that did not matter. With the proper arrangements (bribery and payoffs), the police would accept any story we told them and make it official. Even though he said this, he seemed quite afraid of the police and seemed to be on negative terms with them for some past events unknown to us.

Anna and I looked at each other and realized that we had entered into a local political quagmire and were being squeezed to do something illegal to benefit the hotel owner. What was really going on, we were not sure. Perhaps we had stepped into a big old karma. We did not know how corrupt Hans was, but it was clear that in his twenty years in Guatemala he had learned the game. Whatever the police had on him, it was evident that they were massively corrupt too. I quickly tried to evaluate what we should do and worried that our safety was at stake. Both Anna and I called in our allies and helping spirits—clearly, we were out of our league here.

Once again Hans's wife came over to the table to say that he should just pay us mil dollares so they could all go home and go to bed. He was careful to tell her that he was going to pay us but did not mention any thousand dollars. In his drunken state he had forgotten that we could speak Spanish and knew what his wife had said. After more braggadocio and more indirect threats, he finally got down to it. "How about if I absorb your hotel room cost, pay you four hundred dollars, and pay for your dinner and we call it a night?" he proposed. "You tell the police it happened somewhere else."

A thousand thoughts went through my head. I knew that our trip insurance would not cover lost cash and that all the equipment lost would be depreciated after subtracting a large deductible. The truth is we would end up with nothing. I considered the very limited funds we had left and how much we would need to finish our trip. I was also aware that Hans was by this time very drunk and his character was quite suspect. It would not be good to piss him off or ask him for very much money since, being a young soul, he identified closely with his money and did not want to part with it even if his wife knew they had plenty. But he was also asking us to lie in the report to save his hotel a lot of trouble with the tourism department.

I made my decision. I said, "We have little money left to finish our trip. Our credit card has been stolen so we can't pull any out. We need five hundred dollars to be able to finish our trip. If you give us five hundred and cover our hotel room and the meal tonight, we would really appreciate it, and we will tell the police whatever you want." He replied, "I'll give you four hundred."

I said, "No, we really need five to make our trip happen." I could see the terrible pain in his eyes as he realized he was going to have to part with another hundred dollars. On the other hand, I was not asking for so much that he would consider it worthwhile to make us disappear. At last he agreed but said he did not have the money with him; it was at home. Because I didn't want him to vanish on us, I said we could go to his house on the way to the police station to file the report. As he staggered from the restaurant stone drunk, I prayed it was not far to his house.

The ride was nothing short of terrifying. It was a Saturday night and the streets were filled with revelers and other drunk people. My worst fantasy was that he would run over someone and kill them while we were riding in his car and then we would all end up in a Guatemalan jail to rot or be raped and murdered.

I realized that this was like a passion play somehow unfolding before our eyes. We had stumbled into a series of events that were beyond our control and there was something significant about it that I could not yet fathom. Anna and I had very little opportunity to interact, so mostly we communicated through glances and eye contact. Although on and off terrified on the surface by the dangers of the experience, deep down both of us felt calm, even amused about it. Yes, we were truly having an adventure—perhaps even a misadventure—but I kept thinking that if we survived, it would make a great story.

I was not surprised by the splendor of his estate. As we strolled through the gardens and past a huge swimming pool, he said, "People think I am a wealthy man but I am not really rich." We passed several buildings and when I asked about them, he couldn't help himself. "I have ten large houses here that I rent out in addition to my own house." Despite his fear that we would think he was rich and try to squeeze more money out of him, he felt compelled to report his significant holdings to us. Clearly he was a very wealthy man who came from a well-stationed German family and wanted for nothing. He even made a point of telling us his new Rottweiler puppy had cost over seven hundred dollars and came with papers. We heard a long story about puppy breeders in Guatemala who catered to the wealthy and how he was lucky to get this one for so cheap.

As we entered his home, more Rottweilers came out to greet us along with the biggest German shepherd I have ever seen. Fortunately for us they were friendly but it could have been otherwise if Hans were not with us. There was a pause in his monologue and we waited as he tried to remember why we were at his house. I reminded him about the money he had come to get. Very displeased, he agreed and went to get his wallet, which was stuffed to overflowing with hundred-dollar bills. I will never forget how reluctantly he withdrew five crumbled bills and handed them to me as if he were giving me his last dime. Anna and I kept talking about how wonderful his dogs were, figuring this would distract him and put him in a better mood. He clearly loved his dogs.

As we weaved down to the police station in his car, we had to remind him a couple of times where we were going. When we arrived, we were surprised to find his wife waiting for us. She asked him, "Did you give them the mil dollares?" Evasively, he answered, "I paid them."

The police lieutenant we had been dealing with, sitting in front of his computer, asked me, "Have you come to some kind of agreement?"

"Yes, we have," I replied.

"Is it to your satisfaction?" the policeman asked.

"Yes!"

"Where shall I say it happened, then?"

"On a bus," I said.

He did not blink an eye. After about forty-five minutes Anna and I had completed our separate reports. Hans and his wife drove us back to our hotel—the most dangerous and death-defying ride of all at breakneck speed through the narrow streets—but we made it without smashing into anything. Stunned by the entire episode, we fell into bed at midnight facing a 4:30 A.M. wake-up call for a three-hour shuttle that would take us to Guatemala City followed by a nine-hour bus ride to Tikal.

Anna and I continued to puzzle over this series of events. What the hell was it all about? What were the lessons? What did we miss, if anything? Did we behave properly under the circumstances? I thought so, but one never knows. Maybe I should have refused any money, but then we might not have experienced all that we did. It seemed important that Hans should at least keep his word after promising to compensate us—and as our price for lying for him. The reality is that it was not a lie because the police were completely complicit with it. We were expected to play the game.

Why were the police so upset with Hans? What did they have on him, and what was he paying to be left alone? The mystery remained with us for the rest of trip. One thing was clear, however. We had run into a very wealthy young soul who was profoundly insecure and identified solely with his money. He was deeply unhappy, filled with rancor, revenge, and hatred. He was involved in a corrupt way of life and, when faced with a threat to his security, would resort to almost anything to regain control. And yet in a childish sort of way, he felt compelled to at least partially keep up the appearances of honorableness.

Even so, we both found it possible to forgive him his short-comings and recognize him as a face of Spirit, just a confused one. In fact, the police and all the characters in the play were also faces of Spirit that were helping us to learn something important. It was okay.

A week later we were home safe and sound but a little worse for wear. We hit the ground running as usual, immediately leading a five-day retreat at Eagle Bear Ranch. Both of us agreed that the event was not quite over; there would be more. Maybe it would have to do with dealing with the trip insurance we had taken out, we thought—but that was not it.

During the beginning of the retreat, Anna dreamed that she was back on the shores of Lake Atitlán and could feel the immense power of the Mayan lake. The lake told her that the robbery was a test and it was not over yet.

Later we did a drum journey and Anna had a sudden, profound, and unexpected experience. When the drumming began, a quetzal, a bright, sacred, Guatemalan bird, showed up and asked her to follow it. She followed the bird as it took her down a very bright tunnel. She traveled for a long way before popping through into a strange, fuzzy, dark place. After looking around and not being able to see her surroundings clearly, she asked the quetzal where he had led her.

"You are at the bottom of the lake," it said.

Remembering her dream about the power of the lake, she said, "What is the source of the power of this lake? I would like to meet it."

The quetzal said, "Look down."

She looked and saw a strange square opening in the lake floor below her, and the quetzal indicated that she had to go down through the opening to find what she was looking for.

Anna asked the quetzal if it was coming with her and it told her that no, she would have to do this part by herself. She bolstered her courage, went down through the strange hole, and popped into a dark, cave-like place. The energy was intense and somewhat scary. Out of the dark came a grotesque, frightening, lizard-like creature that stood staring at her in an intimidating way. She felt like turning and running but instead held her ground and stared back at the creature and announced, "My name is Anna Stevens. I am a daughter of the Great Spirit. I came here because I wanted to know the source of the power of this lake." The creature continued to stare, giving no answer. *Don't worry, nothing can hurt me*, Anna told herself.

Suddenly the creature transformed into an extraordinarily beautiful woman. "Congratulations," she said. "You have passed the test."

With this, Anna felt tremendous relief.

We could not be introduced to the source of this Mayan power place without meeting some kind of a test. Would we freak out? Would we take the events personally? Would we deal with the situation unreasonably or unfairly? Would we whine and complain? What would we do? Apparently we had done what we were supposed to do and played our parts well, and it was through Anna that we found access to the powers of this land.

The beautiful lady spoke again. "Is there anything you would like to ask me?"

"Yes," Anna answered. "Will you agree to protect and support any group we bring down to work with the power places of the Maya in Guatemala?"

"Yes," the woman said.

We had just received an extraordinary gift: protection from any harm for all our travelers for all future trips. This was better than any insurance policy with lots of small print that makes it worthless. For this reason alone, the test had been well worth it, with the bonus of containing many lessons.

I have led two large groups to Guatemala since then, and we have twice gone across Lake Atitlán on motorboats. On the second trip a large windstorm came up and created huge waves that almost scuttled our boat. Yet remembering what the goddess of the lake told Anna, I was never afraid. Everyone got wet, but no one got hurt.

POSTSCRIPT

What were the lessons? As far as I know, they are these:

- Observe and discern but don't judge.

- Forgive everyone as events are unfolding and see all characters in the play as the face of Spirit.

- Treat all characters with respect, no matter what.

- The fact that you have had high times in one place does not necessarily mean you are off the hook for the next place.

- You must form new relationships with the helping spirits of each place and pass their tests if you want something. The helping spirits of the last place will not necessarily be able to help you in the new place. They are for that place only.

- Keep "don't-know mind," a Buddhist expression for "be open to everything."

- It's not over until it's over.

- The catalyst for the lesson is not necessarily the main event. It just sets the play into action.

- What you lose is not important. What you gain is.

- Being in control is not always possible or even desirable, but keeping your wits about you is.

After the trip, Anna told me her video camera had been malfunctioning and it was going to cost a lot to fix, maybe more than it was worth. Instead, it vanished. We recouped half of the thousand dollars. The rest was the price of admission to this misadventure.

There may be more lessons that we don't yet know. Adventures and misadventures can be the gifts that keep on giving.

EXERCISES

Consider a misfortune that you feel you suffered in your life. Did you learn something? What did you learn? What price, if any, did you pay for these lessons? Was the misfortune actually a test? Was it an initiation? Was it worth the price of admission?

◻

Think of a time when you were robbed or ripped off. What were your feelings? Victimization? Anger? Now imagine that you could freely give the robber what they took from you. Just give it to them with blessings. Be in the driver's seat about this. Can you do it? What is that like?

5

ENCOUNTERS WITH THE POWER OF ABORIGINES AND SONGLINES DOWN UNDER

Or "When the Student Is Not Ready"

In October 1998, I had the unique opportunity to go to the outback of central Australia with a group of mixed professionals to visit Aborigines of the Pitjantjatjara tribe. These are people who have been particularly willing to dialogue with outsiders and share their culture and stories. This is the story of my journey and what I learned in that magical and powerful land. Some of it you may find entertaining while other parts of it are unsettling and deeply revealing about human nature and how personality obstacles operate under stress. I have deliberately changed the names of the characters in the story out of respect for the aboriginal people and the professionals' desire to keep certain aspects secret. You will soon learn why.

The trip was to be a meeting of cultures: twelve business consultants to Fortune 500 companies and government departments, keynote speakers, and heavyweights in their fields meeting with aboriginal singers and keepers of the dreamtime songs. The dreamtime is considered by the Aborigines to be the deeper reality behind the world of appearances. For them, specific songs stretch across thousands of miles, embedded in the land itself, narrating the ancient events that have taken place in each location, carrying their significance and meaning. The aboriginals are the carriers of these songs and by singing them they hold the land in balance.

Six women and six men, Americans and Australians, convened at Uluru (Ayers Rock) in the deep red desert of the outback to meet one another and their guides and watch the crimson sunset from the comfort of a balcony in the resort hotel. Included in the group were an internationally recognized economist, six authors, nationally known speakers, two Jungian analysts, an educational specialist, and various business consultants. Joining us were specialists on Pitjantjatjara culture, a translator, guides, drivers, and cooks. We were warned that where we were going there would be primitive facilities, dangerous snakes, and an aboriginal culture so different from our own that, to enter into a dialogue with the indigenous people, we would have to leave behind all expectations and belief systems.

Exhausted from travel and suffering from jet lag, we slipped off to bed after brief introductions. Early the next morning, with some members of the group outfitted with sparkling new and clean desert attire and makeup, we climbed aboard two large four-wheel-drive trucks, outfitted as people and gear carriers, that looked like they meant business. For hours we bounced over the rutted desert roads leading to the deep outback, horizons stretching away in every direction, the flat landscape dotted with shrubs, gum trees, and the occasional rock outcropping.

A brief stop for lunch revealed the first dawning reality of what we were in for: a gum tree forest with flies so thick in the heat of October that we had to eat the sandwiches flies and all. Nervous laughter and fly jokes sputtered among the august group, and with much relief we resumed the journey. The landscape transformed into low rocky mountain ranges and a harsh but colorful desert dotted with spring wildflowers. Large lizards continually crossed the road ahead and feral camels could be spotted among the low trees. The travelers got a chance to converse and get to know one another a bit during the long and dusty ride.

We were tired and gritty from the day's travel, and the new clothes had an even newer layer of red dust and wrinkles. Sweat stained the armpits, hat brims, and collars of many. The neat fabric of Western sophistication was already beginning to fray.

Here for the first time we met our hosts, the aboriginal Pitjantjatjara tribal members who had gathered to meet us at a special place in the dreaming, the songline that this particular "mob" was responsible for keeping alive. *Mob* is the term they themselves use to describe their tribe. They were a dark-skinned people in filthy rags with hair that looked like it had never been washed. Their bare, leathery feet padded about the red earth like gnarled tree roots, making no sound. With bright smiles and warm eyes filled with vitality, they shook our hands. Here we were, twelve Western professionals awkwardly gaping at a ragged, disheveled, and filthy-looking band of Aborigines whose trash littered the ground all around us.

What were we going to do here anyway? How could we possibly bridge the overwhelming chasm between our cultures? One part of me was appalled by these people squatting in the dirt. What was I doing here? Another part of me knew instinctively that these dark people possessed a knowledge so deep, basic, and natural that by comparison our group might as well have been a test-tube creation of left-brained Western science.

After dinner we travelers discussed how we would bridge the gap between us and "them." As a group of professional facilitators, we were good at faux-sharing our feelings and covertly sliding our brilliant observations and insights to impress one another and make points, Western style. The indigenous people just stared at us out of the darkness, watching our council meeting with inscrutable intent.

That night we slept in swags, Australian outback canvas sleeping bags, out under the phenomenal Southern Cross, Magellanic gas clouds, and a Milky Way I had never seen so clearly before. A powerful cold wind whipped up the dust and disturbed our sleep, creating fitful dreams and bringing in the sounds of distant baying dingoes.

The next day we gathered for morning news, an aboriginal tradition focusing on dreams of the night before. We were going to see if our individual dreams might also be collective and speak of our group's relationship to this place. The first dreams were disturbing and indicated conflict and lack of integration. We met with aboriginal elders who spoke of their difficulties: alcoholism, drug abuse, petrol sniffing, and the violence that had all but destroyed aboriginal culture in recent years. As we looked about, we saw no one between fifteen and fifty. Those in the middle generation were all dead, jailed, or living in the slums of the big coastal cities. Great-grandparents were raising the young children, like in the ghetto communities of the United States. Yet there was hope. These children would have the probability of becoming men and women of high degree, carriers of the ancient knowledge—or maybe not if they elected the course their parents followed.

Later that day we walked to a spring in the rocky ridge above camp, a hole in the rock where a solitary pool of water rested overlooking the dry surrounding outback. Lester, an old aboriginal shaman responsible for this site on the songline, told us the story as the old women sang fragments of the story, accompanied by click sticks. This was the site where a great lizard, Kilanta, lay crouched in the time of the ancestors while he contemplated stealing the wonderful stone used by the people in the nearby village for grinding their grain to make bread. He could tell by its sound that the stone was a very fine one and would serve him well if he could just snatch it while they were not looking. Being a shape changer, he began devising ways he could trick the people in order to steal their grinding stone.

Now this episode is only a tiny fragment of a much greater storyline about Kilanta and his adventures that stretch along a songline for thousands of miles across Australia. The many adventures of Kilanta are invisibly written in the rock, the outcroppings, and the caves across the land. These adventures must be told and retold, sung and resung, and in this way they remain alive to teach ongoing generations of people how to live—and how not to. They are sung by the ancestors embedded in the land through the voices of countless generations, bringing them together across time and space. These are the creation stories sung by the land through the voice of the people.

Back in council, the fabric of our little group began to rip apart. Some members complained that they wanted more contact, more discussion with the indigenous people, but expressed frustration that they didn't know how to bring that about. Our translator, a woman, told us we would have to wait, that the indigenous people needed us to live with the land for a time before we could understand anything about them. Members of the group were impatient and there were grumblings. One prima donna in her fifties, a consultant to the U.S. military, could be overheard complaining to others that to sit and wait was not what she came for. She began to show signs of stress and carved out familiar territory, grumbling among the women and complaining that the men were more vocal, running the show, and that the women were somehow getting a raw deal. Some women found themselves caught in the middle, wanting to be on her good side but not quite agreeing. Their makeup was beginning to look smudged and out of place in this raw land of termite mounds, red dirt, and sharp spinifex grass.

The dreams recounted at the morning news session were worrisome. Rain spattered on us as, one by one, members of the group told of headless bodies and other uncomfortable motifs springing up in the night. We discovered from our Australian guides that decapitation is a major theme in the outback. Many white explorers have lost their heads both figuratively and physically over the centuries. Some have been rendered stark raving mad after attempting to cross the outback, and others have been found literally headless, their lifeless bodies sprawled among the carnage of their expedition gear. Had we begun losing ours in some way too? I thought so.

One day the Western women set off to do what the aboriginal women called women's business and left with the translator and the ragged children in tow. We men remained at camp to pursue men's business with our male hosts but with no translation for the day. We might have taken part in a kangaroo hunt, but the women had taken all the vehicles to look for good places to dig honey ants in the bush.

We men gathered with the old ones and noticed that all of us came alive upon being alone together. The old ones immediately began to fashion us red headbands out of woolen yarn to match their own. These signified men's initiation work, and we discovered that these aboriginal elders had taken time out from their important initiation ceremonies with their young men to spend some time with us and make us feel included. We were quite touched and felt a kinship with them. This was beginning to be fun.

The elders taught us the dances of the emu and the powerful dance of the eagle. Over and over we swooped and dove to the sounds of the clicking sticks, and then with a mighty pounce each of us in turn snatched up a rabbit in our talons. We danced, we laughed, we bonded through elation in the smoke of the fire in the middle of a vast land that was beginning to feel strangely like home. The old men's eyes glittered and they spoke in broken English with great warmth. We sat in the dirt in the rain and watched the elders make ceremonial objects.

One man in our group, an old friend of mine, had an illness. He had not been helped by Western medicine and had nearly died during the past year. He requested help from one of the elders, a man of high degree who we had been informed was a healer. Together Kevin and I sat on the earth amid the rubbish of their camp. Frank, an old man with a gray beard, a tattered cowboy hat, and greasy shirt and pants, bade Kevin to take off his shirt so he could examine the problem area. We tried to explain to him that Kevin had had problems with hemorrhaging in the head. I wondered what Frank knew already and what he could see. He was not my picture of a healing shaman, but then when have my Hollywood expectations ever been accurate? Scattered raindrops smacked on our faces and upon Kevin's shirtless Irish white body.

Frank began to massage Kevin's neck, deeply penetrating with gnarled, calloused fingers. His hands massaged expertly into the left side of the neck and down the left arm. He said that the problem was there and he indicated in sign language that he wanted to know what happened to Kevin's left shoulder and arm. Kevin thought for a while and then, with a look of surprise, revealed that as a small child he was left-handed but his school teacher had caned his left hand so hard that he couldn't use it anymore, forcing him to become right-handed. Out here in the outback, Down Under, an old black man unraveled the pain and insanity of a barbaric twentieth-century Western custom. Frank said there was no bad spirit left in there and that it just needed some more healing. He pulled out something bad from the shoulder with his hands, left the circle, and cast it out into the bush.

He returned to massage Kevin's neck and shoulder once more. He said he would do more the following day, ending the session. Kevin was beaming. With a broad grin he excitedly exclaimed, "I've made contact! I've made contact!" And truly he had. I felt the same.

At the end of the day the women returned in a swirl of dust. They had been involved in women's business. They seemed tired and not too happy. Their clothes and bodies were dirty and they didn't have much makeup left. Truth was beginning to reveal their inside state. They saw the men's beaming faces, and several of them demanded to know what we had been doing. We tried to tell them and some of them seemed very put out. Later we found out they had spent the day with screaming children, digging three-foot-deep holes and looking for a few honey ants without much success. The honey ants are a treat, their large abdomens filled with a sweet nectar that can be sucked out. These corporate women had been faced with aboriginal women's work and some of them did not like it at all. They were sure that the men were experiencing something much better, much more important. One of them demanded to see the headman so she could get equal time with him. He was gracious enough to oblige her and spent some time talking to her and several of the women.

At sunset we men were led into the bush. A cold wind was blowing but we were asked to take off our shirts, and one by one the old men painted our bodies with white stripes and dots. They put leaves into our red headbands and chanted prayers as we were transformed into eagles. We emerged from the bush in a long line and performed the dances we had been taught in front of the women and children assembled around a roaring campfire.

We became emus; we became eagles. I have never felt so much like an animal. The prayers, the dances, the ceremony of painting were all working. We felt like men and yet we felt like animals of the land and sky. The dances were sacred, and we were in awe. That night around the campfire we men spoke warmly and openly about our feelings for the land, its magic, and ourselves.

The morning news continued to reveal fragments of unsettling dreams that spoke of trouble in our band. That day we traveled by truck along the songline, stopping at sacred spots to hear more of the story of Kilanta and his ancient travels across this part of central Australia. At each site the Pitjantjatjara sang the song to us and to the land. We saw how the lizard man hid in a cave to avoid detection by the villagers he had stolen from. We heard how he cleaned his beard on the cliff face and vomited up boulders after greedily eating too much in celebration of his theft. Finally, we crawled into his belly, a sacred cave perched high up on a cliff face decorated with art left by generations of people over thousands of years. From the cave, the plain spread before us to the horizon, a beautiful land inviting us to walk out into it.

The songlines and the sacred sites along it evoked powerful emotions and reactions. I felt a strange sadness at the cave, and at our lunch stop I intuitively walked out into the bush where kangaroo, dingo, camel, and emu tracks crisscrossed the baked mud like a mosaic between the termite mounds. I found a huge gum tree and stood under it, looking up at its thick, fragrant branches. I asked it to help me feel more at peace, joyful, and connected. Hearing voices, I wandered over to where Mary, a vivacious aboriginal woman, was digging furiously into the earth searching for honey ants. Her small niece was observing her, and some members of our group were standing nearby taking pictures of her. After a few minutes she handed me a shovel and pointed for me to dig. I labored in the hot sun for a time and then she indicated for me to stop. She reached carefully down with a twig and began to pull out dozens of fat honey ants. Again she dug, burrowing deep into the earth, dirt flying in every direction until, stopping suddenly, she repeated her pattern and pulled out more honey ants. How she knew where they were and when to stop digging I could not fathom. The honey ants piled up in my handkerchief like a mound of gold. We indulged ourselves with a few and then triumphantly carried the rest back to where everyone was just finishing lunch, just in time for dessert.

The aboriginal people grinned broadly at me as I distributed Mary's honey ants, and the rest of our crew shared in the treasure, laughing and slurping. I felt wonderfully connected and then remembered my prayer at the big gum tree and was dumbstruck at the sequence of events. I realized the magic and sacredness of this land. Honored land that is sung to responds quickly and powerfully. In the evening some of us shared our experiences of the day around the campfire. I related my story, and Kevin spoke eloquently about the power he felt in the land, its great beauty, and his awe of it. We had long moments of pregnant silence that we savored in one another's company. I slept under the stars that night, understanding why I had come so far to be here.

But all was not well. Deep, disturbing currents were flowing through elements of our group. The dreams of decapitation revealed a growing rift in our band. At the morning news, it erupted. Kevin, a world-renowned economist and consultant to governments, questioned why we must keep processing the dynamics of our group so much and talking so much. He wanted to be more silent and experience the land and its people more.

In a torrent of venom, one woman viciously attacked him as representing male domination and insensitivity. With much anger she stated that the land was sad, used up, and violated and that there was nothing to gain here. She did not share the joy and the connection of the night before and was furious and unwilling to participate with the group any longer. She went on to attack Kevin's character in a way that left the group stunned and horrified. This woman, well respected in the business world, an author and speaker, had behaved in an uncivilized and atrocious way. We experienced the verbal rape of one of our members and all of us felt abused. The fragile coalition was torn asunder as various men and women in turn stomped off or limped away to lick their wounds.

This group of savvy professional Westerners, espousing the latest theories of cooperation and communication, facilitators of the largest and most powerful corporations on earth, had come apart in conflict and hate. A pall settled over the camp as small knots of former group members whispered together about what had happened and whether there was any way to mend the rip in our community. The Jungians among us proposed that perhaps we were being affected by the dream lines and the songline at this particular place. They suggested that powerful forces were exerting their influences and that we might not be able to explain these events as reactions to simple personal differences. The Australian guides were appalled at the rift between male and female among the Americans and could not understand the depth of rage in the vociferous woman and her supporters. They said they had never seen such anger over such little provocation.

The next day it was time for the women to learn dances and present for the men. Only three of the Western women participated because of the painful and awkward conflict that had arisen. To perform this honey ant dance, it was necessary for the women to bare their breasts, and this was the last straw for three of the women, who refused to participate. So much for the exchange of cultures! The three willing women spent the afternoon ceremonially preparing their bodies. They were accepted into the womb of a canvas tent where they were anointed and fussed over by the elder women. Later these women said it was like coming home to family.

When the men assembled by the fire for the dance, the women, accompanied by an elder, lined up facing the men. They were so painted and decorated that they had lost their individual identities and were totally transformed into honey ants. The other women of the group were nowhere to be seen. The dance was so gentle, so poignant, so beautiful that we men were moved to tears. These women made themselves vulnerable in a way that began to heal some of the wounds of the morning.

Early the next morning we bid our farewell to the Pitjantjatjara, exchanging gifts and smiles. We had connected with them, but at a price. They had suffered out here in this rough land and so had we. They felt the pain of our group but could not heal it. We could not heal it either. Our expectations for talks were not met but we had learned something else, something deeper about ourselves through this land and its people. I looked around at our sunburned faces, our dirty clothes, our disheveled appearance. In a few days we had begun to look more like our hosts. Gone were the polish, the professional veneer, and the pride of a false personality, replaced by a soberness, a more reality-based look.

The truck carried us several hours away to a new encampment, a different songline, and we met the tribal keepers of this land. We walked the land, watched the sunrises and sunsets, listened to the parakeets chirping, and watched them as they flew in great flocks around the rare water holes in the rocks. Parrots and spinifex doves wheeled about the stunning landscape, creating an ever-changing panorama in the sky. Once again we listened to the songs and tales of the land and were stunned, for here was the site of the Seven Sisters songline, the story of the Pleiades.

It was the story of a big, dark, ugly man who was hopelessly attracted to seven beautiful sisters. He followed them over the land, hoping to catch them and have intercourse with them. Being a shape shifter, he was able to disguise himself as a rock or a plant in order to sneak up on them. However, the oldest sister was so perceptive that she always spotted him and led her sisters to safety in the nick of time. This big ugly man had a regular penis and in addition he had a huge, long penis that he wrapped around his waist many times. This long penis had a mind of its own and could unravel at will, darting out to penetrate one of the seven sisters unexpectedly, even when he was not planning to. He tried to get rid of it because of its unruly nature and because it scared the sisters away, but to no avail. Eventually the wayward penis attacked the youngest sister, raped her, and killed her, to the horror of everyone. Her six sisters accompanied her to the sky, where they became the seven stars of the Pleiades. According to the story, the long penis in pursuit of the sisters became Orion's belt and is still following them.

We visited an ancient sacred cave filled with paintings depicting the story I've just retold. The women in our group revealed pain at hearing the story and seeing the images while the men were fascinated with the story and the cave. In the evening several women revealed that they had been raped earlier in their lives.

We pondered whether visiting this songline had precipitated the deep conflict in our group and the intense, unprovoked anger toward the men. Perhaps we were entering the story written in the land and playing it out in some unconscious way. Whatever the case, our rift could not be healed at this time. We met as a group during a fiery Australian sunset and tried hard to make peace with the angry women, to try to look at the anger and understand it, but we could not. The attempt failed utterly and the author and public speaker, the human development specialist, remained grimly silent, unable or unwilling to engage in any kind of healing dialogue.

Although this saddened the rest of our group, we were able to look at one another—dirty, ragged, smoke stained, and wind burned—and see greater depth than before. We looked better than when we had first met, eyes glittering, vitality exuding, mouths smiling. We were about to go home having been initiated, rendered more compassionate, transformed in ways beyond our understanding. We had gone through hardship and emotional strain, had old wounds opened by this land and its people. We were sobered and humbled and the emperor's clothes were strewn across the landscape.

These thought leaders (or perhaps thoughtless ones) had arrived competitive and prideful, filled with silly expectations, and we had utterly failed our mission. What we gained was immeasurably more valuable—we were humbled, and these ragged unwashed people had taught us deeply in nonintellectual ways. They could not fix us and we could not fix them. They have terrible problems to overcome if they are to survive as a race. Yet their problems, however difficult, are not more challenging than the ones we faced. We were unable to make it through a week without a social meltdown. What does that say for our communities and society? What does that say about our leaders?

When we returned to Uluru I walked around but did not climb it out of deference for the Aborigines who requested that we not do so. For them it is a great power place. I could feel that it was. It is the *apu*, to use a term from the Quechua language of the Incas: the guardian for all the outback, the aboriginal lands. Since the white man came and turned it into a tourist attraction, it has been somewhat desecrated, not unlike what has happened to Mount Everest. The Aborigines have suffered, but they await the time when they can have it back. Perhaps then their situation will shift for the better.

Upon returning home I had much to ponder, much to under-stand about the relationships between the masculine and the feminine. Since the songlines are thousands of years old, the rift between the masculine and feminine is very old as well. These songlines are meant as teaching songs. Lizard man is each of us, whether male or female. He is our lower nature, our sim-ian nature. The seven sisters are the seven chakras connected to our higher nature. The lower nature attempts to bring down the higher nature and sometimes succeeds, but not completely or forever. All we have to do is look up into the sky and recall the story to remind us of this. Lizard man may catch one of us once in a while, but according to the story he does not catch all of us. Therein lies our salvation.

I now look at the Aborigines from Australia in a very differ-ent light because they revealed themselves to me through their songs, through their wisdom, through the grubs they shared with me, and through their patience with us. I am so blessed.

POSTSCRIPT

It has been some years since this trip. Sometimes I catch my travel companions in the news plying their trade. Except for Kevin, my old soul friend, I don't know how they have evolved. That is not for me to judge. Some were ready to heal and some were not. I still regard this trip as one of the signature events of my life.

Sometimes a bid for power will strip off your pretty clothes and set you naked in the elements where the truth can be seen. Resistance is futile but at the time it seems like a safe option. Acceptance is the only way through, although it may look like weakness to others. Don't take it personally. It is their own fear of being weak being projected onto you.

Never accept appearances. That lesson keeps popping up over and over in these stories. I guess it is one I need to learn big time.

QUESTIONS

Have you ever gone into something with high expectations only to have the situation melt down and become a kind of disaster? If so, who did you blame? Yourself? Others? Did you learn anything? From your perspective, did you emerge more powerful or not?

PART II

INSPIRATION
Ceremonialist-Healer

The stories in part II have the central theme of healing accompanied by ceremony (or in some cases without ceremony). A ceremony is sacred time set aside to perform actions that bring about transformation for those participating. Some ceremonies are about initiations, some are to mark sacred time frames, and others are for the purpose of facilitating someone's healing. A shaman ceremonialist is capable of carrying out either a spontaneous ceremony or one that has the force of tradition behind it.

A shaman healer can bring back harmony and balance among the various forces of nature, restoring resonance between the sick person and Spirit, from whom they have felt cut off. Of course, each one of us is our own best healer and thus the shaman is only a catalyst for that healing, yet an important one. Every good shaman knows that it is not they themselves who heal. The power of Spirit acting through them accomplishes this. Healers diagnose, use allies to conduct extraction techniques, bring back connection and wholeness, and cast out demons, whether physically manifested or perceived. Without the cooperation of the patient, the healer has no power to heal.

6

Q'EROS

Encountering the Power
of the Land and Its People

During October 2009, I had the extraordinary opportunity to travel from the Peruvian Andes to the Amazon jungle, visiting first the Q'ero people in the mountains and then the Shipibo of the upper Amazon. This amazing trip was only partially the result of long-term planning. While the trip to the jungle was on our schedule, the Andean part was last minute.

One of our students, Richard, had connected with the Q'ero on a prior trip to Cusco and had become godfather to our guide Torribio's daughter Angelita. The child was now close to two years old, and it was time for the important haircutting ceremony that signals an infant's initiation into the community. Because of high infant mortality, it is unclear whether children will even survive. Until age two, despite whether the child is male or female, their hair remains uncut and uncombed and can appear quite scraggly. Being the godparent, Richard was expected to go to Peru, cut Angelita's hair, and give the proper gifts and financial support. He did not particularly want to make this challenging trip alone and had asked my daughter, Anna; my wife, Lena; and me if we would be interested in going. After brief consideration, we decided that this was an unparalleled opportunity to visit a people we were very much interested in meeting, so we responded with an unqualified yes.

As if by magic, Richard met Carrie, an American woman in Cusco who spoke Quechua and had worked extensively with the Q'ero for more than four years. Her home had become the informal meeting place for the Q'ero during their visits to Cusco. Not only was she very helpful in helping plan the trip, but she agreed to go with us and translate. She helped put together all the complex arrangements for horses, a cook, and staff to accompany us on a trip that would carry us to between eleven thousand and sixteen thousand feet. In the end, our team included Richard; Anna and her husband, Aaron; Aaron's sister Rachel; Lena and me; and of course Carrie. According to spiritual archetypes, this team included two scholars (Anna and me), one warrior (Richard), one artisan (Lena), two sages (Aaron and Rachel), and one king (Carrie), making for a well-rounded team. Fortunately, the staff included servers, warriors, and artisans, so we were balanced out with expression, inspiration, action, and assimilation role types, the same mapping used for this book. Since we met priests along the way, all role types were represented in some way.

We spent a couple of days in Cusco to acclimate, and while there I stopped by a street vendor who had a tray of exquisite stones from the region. I bought several, including one beautiful and amazing crystal—actually two crystals joined at the base and covered in extraordinary white calcite. This stone felt so good in my hand that I just had to buy it even though weight was a consideration.

We outfitted ourselves with cold-weather gear, although afterward we were headed for the jungle where it would all be useless.

Then one crisp morning we crowded into a van along with our accompanying cook and several Q'ero assistants for the six- to seven-hour ride southeast from Cusco toward Ausangate, one of the most powerful apus, or sacred mountains, in all of Peru.

The Q'ero's land is remote, just south of Ausangate in extraordinarily steep and rugged mountainous terrain, so rough that until recently it had no roads. The same route is traveled by thousands of people every year going to the Q'oyoriti festival, the most sacred of all the Andean festivals, which takes place in June. After driving over a rugged fifteen-thousand-foot pass on a narrow dirt road through extraordinarily beautiful terrain, we camped for the night at the place where we would begin our trek into Q'eros, land of the Q'ero.

The Q'ero live in a collection of communities in the heights of the Andes. There are many other Quechua-speaking peoples with similar traditions all over the Andes, but the Q'ero have earned a reputation for keeping the original Incan traditions alive and are the go-to people for learning the powerful ways of the shaman ("paqo" as they are called in the Andes). While the Q'ero are willing to share their knowledge with all who are interested, they are quite private when it comes to allowing visitors into their terrain. We were made to understand that only six or seven outside groups per year had permission to enter and travel in Q'eros; would-be visitors cannot go there without special permission and they will be turned back if they have not obtained legitimate entry. Thus, we felt much gratitude for our good fortune to have this opportunity, especially in the company of Carrie, a woman well known to the people as one of their supporters and helpers.

In Cusco, Anna had developed a sore throat and bad cough. Although we tried our best to keep it from spreading, by the time we began the actual trek, Aaron had come down with it and I had a burgeoning sore throat on the first day riding the horses. This did not bode well for a trip to such cold and altitude, and a part of me was very concerned because the symptoms were alarmingly like the swine flu going around in the States. I worked very hard to take my mind off fearful thoughts and focused on leaving it all to Spirit to handle. Eventually the fever and cough spread to Richard as well but no further, so those of us who had symptoms were exactly those who were supposed to.

Despite my illness, the trip was so amazingly beautiful and powerful that I was able to override the symptoms and enjoy myself in the extraordinary altered state that came with high altitude, powerful terrain, and fever. We visited isolated communities, collections of stone houses with grass roofs surrounded by huge herds of llamas and alpacas. Being above tree line, the terrain is barren and rocky, with strange thick mists swirling down around the jagged peaks, sometimes completely obscuring everything before lifting to reveal exquisite mountainous terrain. Without a guide one could easily get lost and die at these altitudes, something the Q'ero warn about and that happens to those who are not invited.

Eventually we came to Torribios's village nestled in a rugged valley surrounded by huge apus all around. Here we participated in a wonderful *despacho* ceremony. In a despacho, many items are gathered together in a special arrangement, prayed over, and burned as an offering to the spirits of the land. There are hundreds of different kinds of despachos, but this was a simple one of gratitude and a request for safe passage. During the ceremony a severe thunderstorm came barreling up the valley and headed directly for us. Large raindrops fell around us and the thunder rolled ominously. An old grizzled Q'ero pulled out his coca leaves and, making a *quintu*, holding three leaves like a fan, he faced the storm and began praying semiaudibly. Within minutes the rain had stopped and the storm changed direction. The old

Q'ero gave us a wide, toothless grin. The clouds lifted to reveal the expansive beauty of the land.

I couldn't help but notice that the offering had an immediate impact on the weather and conditions of the mountains. The paqos of this region know their trade and have power way beyond what we may think is possible; they are known for their supernatural abilities such as altering the weather, teleportation, becoming invisible, conducting alchemy, and performing miracles of healing. Some Q'ero shamans have the responsibility for helping balance the energies of the entire planet, but these subjects are way beyond the scope of this story.

In this village we participated in a haircutting ceremony for Torribio's brother's child. Modesto, Torribio's brother, is also a paqo. A wonderful, humble man who in his childhood had been hit by lightning and injured, he has hip displacement and walks with a severe rolling gate that makes his ability to navigate the mountains improbable. Nevertheless, several days later we met him miles away, ambling along as if nothing hindered him at all.

During the haircutting ceremony, the paqos singled out Lena as the chief participant and made much of her presence, giving her gifts and fawning over her. I have seen this pattern repeated many times over the years: indigenous peoples love Lena and not only respond to her favorably, but often elevate her and recognize her for her power. On the other hand, they usually ignore me altogether and I feel completely overlooked until I earn their respect over a long period of time. While I was used to this pattern, I was surprised to see that I was still bothered by the havoc it played with my self-esteem and the old feelings of self-deprecation that arose. I wanted to celebrate the powerful occasion and rise above these petty feelings I thought I had left behind, but try as I might I was plagued by the same old pattern, especially under the influence of fever and flu. I allowed myself to feel diminished and shunted aside, clear evidence that I had not cleared away enough of my own personal baggage yet.

Lena was being honored, and my scholarly introversion relegated me to the sidelines. I felt fatigue, anger, resentment, self-loathing, and a host of other very unwelcome feelings that I wished would vanish forever, made worse by the fact that I knew these were all projections and had nothing to do with what was actually happening. I longed for an open heart and I got one that was shut down tightly. I could not escape my old process, especially here in Q'eros where nothing could hide. This was exactly what my teacher Guadalupe warned me about: a tendency to feel sorry for myself that got in my way of progress. I knew it and I could see it clearly. I became determined to come to some kind of emotional neutrality and because of my intent I managed a modicum of success. With a supreme effort I "put it all down," as my old Zen master and teacher, Seung Sahnime, used to suggest.

After the haircutting was over, Modesto looked around and asked, "What should her name be?" Prior to this ceremony, children in Q'eros go without a name, strange as that may sound. My monkey mind having subsided, I instantly got her name in my mind. It was Luminosa and I said it out loud. Everyone looked at each other and nodded their heads, knowing this was her name. Modesto said, "Luminosa" and nodded in agreement. And now there is a strong warrior girl growing up in Q'eros with the bright name of Luminosa.

This simple experience shows how quickly the mind can be cleared of its cobwebs and directly tune in. The secret is to be ruthless about energy leaks and deprive them of any indulgence, any mental food whatsoever. This requires much practice but if I had any doubt about whether it was worth it, there is no question as to the difference between indulgence and zero tolerance.

According to the Q'ero, the mountains are filled with spirits and powerful apus who guard and look after their communities.

One has to be very watchful of one's thoughts while traveling through these regions because they may attract either good fortune or dangerous outcomes. I can say that my own experience there verifies what the Q'ero say. My most difficult challenges came at night as I struggled with my health fears and other subconscious material that seemed to be dredged up by the rugged mountains. Deep insecurity, self-deprecation, anger, and victimhood all visited me in the middle of the night at camps sometimes exceeding fifteen thousand feet. From my conversations with the others, I realized I was not the only one having these challenges. Whatever needs to be cleared tends to get pried loose and causes havoc on its way out. Strange dreams seemed to characterize the nights, along with visitations from mountain spirits appearing as old Q'ero men or women, rock creatures, or crystalline beings bearing messages. Lena and Anna had amazing visitations from these apu beings along the way.

One night we made camp at a very high (about sixteen thousand feet) and extremely cold pass amid the peaks. We pitched our tents, had a warm dinner, and turned in very early. I slept soundly until I felt Lena poking me and saying, "José, José, wake up. Look outside." I reluctantly sat up and poked my head out into the freezing night. There was a major light show going on. Although the sky was absolutely clear and the stars shone brightly, great columns of light were rising up from the peaks all around us, flashing on and off. I had never seen anything like that and have not since. It was as if a huge lightning storm was going on but there were no clouds. After a time the cold overcame me and I crawled back into my bag and fell deeply asleep to an epic dream.

Lena did so as well and had a very interesting experience that she describes as partly asleep and partly awake. A great rock being made its presence known to her and indicated that it was looking for *hoocha*. Now, hoocha is the name the Q'ero give to anything that is not resonant with one's well-being. They don't say it is negative, just that it is not in harmony. It is similar to the term used in the jungle, *mal aire*, roughly translated as "bad air" or "negative energy." She watched this great rock being go from tent to tent opening its big jagged mouth and eating the hoocha, our disharmonious thoughts coming from it. In the morning she spoke to the Q'ero about what she had seen and they verified exactly what that being was and what it looked like. Interestingly, I awoke feeling that my mind was clear of all the junk that had been passing through it. I am glad something considered it a good meal.

After several days we arrived at the Q'ero festival site, located in a huge beautiful area where five valleys converged. We had dropped in altitude and the weather was clear and warm. We camped for two nights, and I welcomed the chance to rest. Here also we were invited to climb up to some Incan ruins high above our camp where we held another despacho ceremony and were invited to sing as part of it. Although I was terribly feverish at this point, I sang my heart out and cried at the beauty of the occasion. Later we were told that no outsiders had ever been invited to this particular place before, and we all felt awe for the good fortune that had come upon us. Among the many apus that surrounded us were the two that the Q'ero regard as balancing the whole world.

That night I succumbed to a severe fever and crashed in my tent, sweating furiously throughout the night. I no longer had fight in me, and strangely all my fears left me as I just lay sweating and gave up all resistance to being sick. I figured the mountains and the apus would have their way with me and there was no use fighting them off anymore. The next morning, although very weak, I felt amazingly better and remained so for the rest of the trip. I had passed another major initiation, a process of terrible self-confrontation.

Sometimes these adventures are not what they appear to be to others. They are not all fun and games—I never know what is going to arise. The good part is that the scenery is usually pretty good while I go through whatever comes to the surface to be processed. We experienced so many things with the Q'ero; I can recount only a few of them in this story. As you shall see, in retrospect the trip happened exactly the way it was supposed to.

¤

After returning to Cusco, we prepared ourselves for the radical shift to the Amazon jungle, where we would meet with the Ravens, our two-year-program study group, for intense ceremonies with the Shipibos. We flew to Iquitos and welcomed the heat and humidity of the jungle after the icy cold of the Andes where we had to chip ice off our tents' rainflies every morning. After a day in Iquitos visiting the markets, we loaded onto a river ferry for the six-hour trip to the jungle outpost along the Yarapa River. There, across from the indigenous village of Yarapa, we participated in an intense series of ceremonies overseen by Enrique and Herlinda, our Shipibo teachers and friends.

During the ferry ride we were treated to one of the most beautiful sunsets I can remember. The great cumulonimbus clouds forked out lightning all around as one by one they turned orange and then pink in the sunset. The blue sky turned indigo, and stars began to reveal themselves. I felt a great weight lift off my shoulders and an ineffable happiness surround and penetrate me. I could not remember being so happy in a long time and felt that I had truly come home, surrounded by people I love.

While the Andes are barren, rugged, and masculine, the jungle is succulent, damp, and intensely green, a lowland feminine polar opposite to the heights of the mountains. In the jungle we lay in hammocks throughout the heat of the day and sang out the nights in ceremony. I felt the power of the apus down-loading into me during the ceremonies night after night. After a week we arose at 3 A.M. for a boat trip and bus ride back to Iquitos. Where we had started with sunset on the ferry going to Yarapa, we ended with sunrise on the Amazon, a time of great flying birds, cool breezes, and early morning mists.

We flew to another bustling mestizo jungle town, Pucallpa, where our group would divide. Some members of the group were returning to Lima for the flight home, and the rest would go on to San Francisco, the Shipibo village where we would continue to work with Enrique and Herlinda. There we would diet intensely with specific jungle teacher plants for another ten days. These plants would bestow upon us their knowledge and healing powers. Another group from the States would meet us there to diet as well.

San Francisco was very hot and without rain, so our dieting was rendered more severe: we could not drink water from early morning until close to four in the afternoon. Each morning we would trudge off in the nearby jungle to a beautiful *maloka*, a ceremonial temple with a high palm frond roof, to drink our various plant potions and spend the day in hammocks, processing the plants. Some in our group were just starting their diets with tobacco while others had completed tobacco on former trips and had moved on to *reneqia, boasca, albahaca, camalonga, chiric sanango, cerromacho,* and *marosa.* We took each plant for seven to eight days before moving on to the next. All of these plant drinks contain some tobacco, the foundation plant for all of them.

I was finishing up boasca and beginning camalonga, a cam-phor plant that tasted rather like mothballs but gave a powerful pattern of protection when working with serious diseases and dysfunctions in other people. While the plant is not at all hallu-cinatory, it produces a kind of deep reverie or state of meditation that lasts many hours. Some of that time can be spent meditating, reading, or listening to music on an iPod. Each day I read a little from the works of Patanjali, Gregg Braden's *Fractal Time*, and Tom Kenyon and Judi Sion's *The Magdalen Manuscript* about the balance of masculine and feminine.

On this day, as usual, I set up my mesa on the floor next to my hammock. It consists of a woven woolen cloth containing various healing stones I had received in Q'eros, accompanied by my pipe, Agua Florida, and feathers. The Q'ero paqos mostly use stones in their mesas because this is what is in their environment: a masculine set of tools. The Shipibos use plants because that is what they have in their environment, mostly feminine tools, although there are exceptions to both. I decided to marry the two, stones and plants, and use both during my dieting. I could lean out of my hammock and pick up various stones to contemplate during my day of dieting with a plant, an experiment that produced far-reaching outcomes and big downloads of information.

On the fifth day of the camalonga diet and my seventh overall day, I received a particularly big dose of the brew from Herlinda, who chuckled as she handed me the glass. She sang over me and blew an icaro into my tobacco and Agua Florida as she and the other shamans did every morning. Getting it down was rough, and I had to chase it with a drop of Agua Florida to avoid instantly purging it.

I did an hour of meditation while sitting and then, unable to sit up any longer, retired to my hammock as the heat soared and sweat poured from my body. To get the most mileage, I used some self-hypnosis to go deeper than ever. I received the message that I should pick up the connected crystals covered with calcite that I had purchased in Cusco and place them on my *tan tien* (navel). Instantly I was led to contemplate the imbalance of my masculine and feminine sides.

Now, it is worth noting that several days earlier in ceremony I had asked the shaman to work on balancing my right and left sides because I had been having problems with my left side: an earache on the left, a stuffed-up sinus on the left, an ache in my left shoulder, and so on. These were chronic conditions I'd had for years.

I received an internal message to count back lifetimes to find the one where these conditions started. I counted back and at twenty-seven I saw a miserable man who abused women out of fear of them and loathing for himself. This life was truly terrible and left my psyche with long-term scars and a decision that I simply could not forgive myself for what I had done. A pattern of lifetimes began where I could not get comfortable with the feminine, and the imbalance grew. Feeling such guilt and not forgiving myself created the dynamic that the feminine within me was slowly shriveling up and dying from neglect. I saw that the woman on the left side of my body was shrunken and abandoned, desperate for nourishment, love, and protection. The male side was equally wounded and could not make progress without his other side, which he was so afraid of. They lay in my body, side by side, wounded and unable to communicate, stuck in a stalemate. I was shown that the decision to heal this situation was mine alone. I could neglect it and it would continue, or I could set things right and hop on the road to healing. I could make no more progress on my spiritual path without moving on this.

I contemplated the desperate plight of each side and felt the deepest compassion and sorrow. No one was to blame; both sides were just stuck in time. Since the male needs to move first with action, I reached over with my right hand and gently held my left hand, a first step in reconciliation. At first the left hand was frozen, but little by little each side had many things to say to the other, and as they did so they forgave each other.

Each side was desperate for the love of the other, and with time they moved toward each other with great desire and determination. This process took a number of hours and was deeply and powerfully moving.

After much work had been done, I was told to look at the two connected crystals I had been holding on my tan tien. One was longer and clearly the male; the other was shorter and clearly the female. The longer one looked as if it were protecting the shorter one. In actuality they were one. I was told it was no accident that I had bought this stone; this had been arranged by my essence far in advance. I was then shown the grand scale of events that culminated in this healing of my two sides. First came the trip to the Andes, Q'ero land of stones and the masculine. There, of course, I got sick because the masculine side of myself was sick from being isolated from the feminine. All my demons arose there because they needed purging. I repeated the pattern of feeling overshadowed by the power of the feminine, represented by Lena's being so welcomed by the Q'ero and my feeling overlooked. This was the guy from twenty-seven lifetimes ago rising up with his pain.

The next step was to go to the jungle, the great dark feminine, where I felt overjoyed and where such intense work had to be done. The life-giving moisture and succulence of the feminine were like manna to my soul and my feminine side. I prompted my intellectual center with readings from *The Magdalen Manuscript*, which my old friend Pat had given me. Clearly, she was in on my healing conspiracy as well. Herlinda, a woman shaman, gave me the huge dose of camalonga to push through the big internal work I had to do that day. Under subconscious guidance, I picked up the "marriage crystal" and worked with it without knowing why. My inner guidance laughed at the grand scale of the plan that had been carried out under my nose without my catching on until the very end.

Spirit revealed to me in no uncertain terms that my personality is not in control of my life and is the last to know what is happening. Also, what I have learned to call reality is actually just a big passion play, an elaborate dreamscape where I can act out grand-scale dramas of getting lost and finding my way home again over what appears like many, many lifetimes but is actually just the blink of an eye. What other dreams are being played out even as I write this?

What dreams and dramas are being played out under your very nose that you have failed to notice because you are as caught up in the details of your life as I have been? Better start chuckling now.

POSTSCRIPT

Like the events in this story, the large-scale events of the planet—the imbalances of climate, economies, religious strife, political events, and so on—are just a big drama unraveling for the collective, to teach us in a way that we may learn in order to wake up. They are dreams orchestrated by parts of ourselves so much more powerful and wise than our surface personalities. All is well and all will be well because we are in very good hands. Our job is simply to see, listen, and respond willingly to what we are shown. There is only healing to do and absolutely nothing to fear.

As has happened so many times before, powerful lessons were unfolding within me, and my personality was the last to know. When I was feeling stuck I was actually involved in a bigger drama designed to reveal specific life lessons and solutions to the test I was passing through.

QUESTIONS

How are you being tested right now, or how have you been tested recently? Did you pass this initiation? Are you passing it now? Isn't it time to handle it once and for all? What does handling it look like?

Your ego wants you to think that you have made no progress and never will. It wants you to identify with failure. You might want to take a good look at this. Is that acceptable to you? Always give yourself wiggle room to grow. How are you different? How have you changed? What is not the same anymore?

7

JOURNEYS FOR POWER
WITH MEDICINE
Visions with Ayahuasca

Lena, Anna, and I have been traveling to Peru for more than twenty years to study and learn from the Shipibo tribe in the upper Amazon jungle. They are a tribe of about twenty-five thousand people living in small villages on the Ucayali River system. Over the years, we have worked with a variety of shamans and ayahuasqeros there, for better or for worse. An ayahuasqero is a specialist in working with the plant combination known as ayahuasca, and singing the icaros or sacred songs that guide them in ceremony. We started out working with a Frenchman and from him were led to others and eventually to a set of Shipibo teachers.

I first met Pierre Materez in my hometown of Santa Fe, where he had been summoned by the son of an elderly woman who was suffering from leukemia. As a powerful healer and ayahuasqero, Pierre spent several weeks treating this woman with plants collected in the jungles of Peru. According to the most recent reports, her well-being had greatly improved.

A friend invited my wife and me to have dinner with Pierre and some other friends who wanted to meet him. Upon being introduced to Pierre, who was slight of build, with brown hair and kind but intense eyes, I immediately recognized him as a man of integrity, a quiet man of knowledge, someone I could trust and learn from. He was a very dedicated healer with a strong reputation who worked as a shaman with indigenous Peruvians, mestizos, and visitors from other countries.

Over dinner Pierre told us a little about life in the Amazon region of Peru and his work as a *curandero* (healer). He talked about some of the experiences that had led him to that region to find and develop his botanical gardens. He had been a seeker from a young age, traveling around his native Europe, India, and the United States in his search for knowledge and spiritual truth. He learned much and eventually settled in his adopted country of Peru to grow, study, and catalogue the healing plants of the jungle and the time-honored methods of preparing them for maximum benefits.

For over thirteen years Pierre was apprentice to Benito Masteras, a high-level shaman among the Shipibo and Connibo peoples, and for five years to Miguel and Guillermo Fanela, a father-and-son team, also shamans to indigenous peoples. With them he learned to collect, prepare, and work with many different plant medicines. He learned about the diets that go with ingesting the various plants and learned the icaros that are sung to awaken the plants and activate their healing properties. He also learned the potentially harmful effects of many plants and how to prepare them in a manner that eliminates their toxic effects while preserving their healing potential.

After meeting Pierre in Santa Fe, I had the good fortune to visit him in Pucallpa, a jungle town in Peru's Amazon River basin, in November 1996 with my family and a group of thirty of our students as we traveled to Machu Picchu and other sacred sites.

We participated in healing ceremonies with him outdoors at his botanical gardens, an experience that I can only describe as remarkable and life changing. During these ayahuasca ceremonies, I physically saw the web of life that connects all life forms in the jungle. I could see the origin of the intricate Connibo and Shipibo designs used to decorate objects of art and clothing in this part of the Amazon. I saw how Pierre and his assistants used singing and hand movements to manipulate and repair the fragmented lines forming the web around the patients being healed. As I looked up into the night sky I saw the brilliant illumination of the Peruvian Divine Spirit in the form of Wiracocha smiling benevolently down upon us through the moon-soaked clouds.

During that trip, I recognized that Pierre was held in the highest regard by the local people who came to him for healing. He was gracious and attended to every detail of our stay. I was deeply impressed by the dedication with which he planted his garden, his preparation for ceremony, and his mastery of healing with the plants at his disposal.

I asked Pierre how he came to settle there. He replied that he had been searching throughout the region for the right place to set up a garden and his healing center. He wanted to learn about and preserve the ancient knowledge of plant medicines that is being rapidly lost as Western civilization invades the Amazon. He found an overgrown and neglected garden that already contained many native plant species. He planted many new species and built a center with a cookhouse, a central building with several sleeping bungalows, outhouses, and shower stalls, doing much of this work with his own hands and with the help of local craftsmen. He published a number of books and journal articles in Spanish, focusing on the local flora and its many uses, and he received many guests, including scientists from around the world who were interested in healing plants. One year he was filmed for a segment on plants that aired on Brazilian and Peruvian television.

Over the ten years prior to meeting Pierre, Lena and I had the extraordinary opportunity to lead groups of travelers to sacred power places around the world. After meeting Pierre in Santa Fe, we decided that we must put together a trip to Peru to visit him in the jungle and see the sacred sites at Machu Picchu, Cuzco, Lake Titicaca, and Nazca. Now we were with a group of some thirty travelers including our children, Anna and Carlos, journeying to Peru. Our first destination was Pucallpa, where we would meet with Pierre and participate in ceremonies at his botanical gardens. Our group also included some of our best friends and many people whom Lena and I had known for years. In the group was Ron, a best friend from first grade, tall and laid back, who worked as a wildlife inspector in Los Angeles; Pat, of Irish-Huichol descent, a reserved speech therapist from Marin County whose children had grown up with ours from birth; Joan, a tall, striking psychotherapist friend from San Francisco; Sarah Chambers, the original Michael Teachings channel; and an assorted group of people from every walk of life, including one woman from Iceland. After our trip to the jungle to visit with Pierre, we would be met by nearly ten more people for the remainder of the trip, but this first group was the die-hard crew who wanted to experience the shamanism of the Amazon.

We flew over the mountains to Pucallpa, sailing over the vibrant green and mists rising from the forest canopy of the upper Amazon River basin. Rivers snaked around in huge, lazy curves, their bends almost meeting but kept apart by narrow strips of jungle. As we approached Pucallpa, bright red streaks became roads slashed into the jungle converging on this sprawling jungle town. At the airport we joined Pierre, who was organizing everyone into dilapidated vans and taxis for the short trip to the gardens.

When we arrived he showed us to our sleeping quarters in clean, elevated huts with thatched roofs made of palm fronds. The huts smelled of hardwood and creosote, a necessary anti-rot ingredient in this damp climate. After settling in, we gathered as a group for an early supper and an orientation to the grounds and the next few days' activities. The next day we would participate in our first ayahuasca ceremony in an outdoor hut specially set up for healing work. The hut had an earthen floor and pillars around the outside holding up the thatched roof. Suspended overhead was an enormous length of ayahuasca vine with rough, brown bark and beautiful spirals in its many sections. We would fast in the afternoon so our stomachs would be empty and prepared for taking the ayahuasca.

I turned in early and awoke in the morning to the songs of hundreds of unfamiliar birds in this garden paradise. I spent the day hanging around the gardens and taking a short trip to town to visit some stores and get acquainted with the area. As evening fell, I felt the anticipation of the powerful ceremony that was about to take place. For many in our group it would be the first time taking ayahuasca, one of the more famous of the visionary plant teachers of the Amazon. I had become familiar with its effects but had never taken it in its home in the jungle. I knew that this would be a special experience.

We waited until about 9 P.M. to begin the ceremony so that the last flight at the nearby airport had left and night had fallen. We took our places around the walls of the ceremonial hut, and I suggested that each person form an intention for what they wanted to accomplish. One by one each participant voiced their hopes and fears and stated their intention for the evening. Although several had decided at the last minute not to participate, both my children were looking forward to their first experience with the sacred plants. I could tell they were nervous, but I was very proud of them for their courage and their willingness to try something new.

The ayahuasca was served up as a tea, and one by one each person drank down the sweet-bitter beverage. I sat back in the darkness of the hut with the others to await the inner visions. After about two hours it was clear to me from the sighs and moans that people were already experiencing the effects of ayahuasca. Yet I was feeling very little except lightheadedness. Pierre came around to ask me how I was doing, and I told him I was fine but feeling very little. He asked me if I wanted to take some more and I said yes. He poured another cup and I drank down the tea with a grimace. Almost before I got back to my pad, the visions suddenly began in earnest.

Before long Pierre came around again to see how I was doing. I could barely sit up in front of him while he began to sing icaros and do his healing work with me. Without warning I had the most intense desire to vomit, fell back to a pit around the wall of the hut, and became violently ill. The purge was difficult but deeply satisfying at the same time. I felt I was getting rid of long-held tension and old emotional baggage that I no longer wanted to carry around with me. Following the purge I lay back and could not move a muscle while brilliant streams of colors and energy coursed through my body. Gradually I became aware of millions of points of light in the formerly dark hut, lighting it up so that I could see everything quite well.

After taking the second dose of ayahuasca, not only did I vomit but I realized the medicine was working on my bowels as well. This presented a problem because the outhouses were some distance from the ceremonial hut. Reaching them required a walk down a muddy path overhung by giant plants and trees and then taking a fork to another, fainter path that eventually led to the pit toilet. To remain seated was not an option for too much longer, but to get up and traverse the paths inebriated on ayahuasca seemed like a monumental task. The inevitable forced me to my feet, and I stumbled out into the dark to find the right path leading to my destination where I could relieve myself. I found that my headlamp was quite useless because its weaving beam was such a distraction that I could not see where I was going.

Normally when ingesting ayahuasca, the process is to follow the visions and inner landscapes with eyes closed, but upon opening them an amazing effect takes place. The ayahuasca reveals the webs of consciousness connecting earth and sky, people and plants, and everything within the external visual field. To walk on ayahuasca is like navigating through many thick veils and curtains of latticework. The effect is quite beautiful but a bit disconcerting. I found that I automatically stretched my arms and hands in front of me to penetrate through the beautiful veils, sort of like going through the wardrobe in *The Chronicles of Narnia*, only the terrain was jungle, not snow. The plants, dripping with moisture, were vibrating with life, and pools of scattered, shifting moonlight decorated the ground, the clouds allowing the moon to peek out from time to time. Hundreds of fireflies hung in the branches of the tallest trees accompanied by the sound of the steady dripping of the plants into the puddles below. The air felt thick, and the fragrance of flowers perfumed the warm damp breeze. I was truly in another land.

For what seemed like centuries, I staggered on a path that hours earlier had been completely familiar but now passed through an incredibly beautiful alien world. I could not recognize anything but continued down the footpath and then followed a fork. Eventually I made it to one of the outhouses but was confronted with a massive spider the size and shape of a tarantula that squatted directly in the entrance. Realizing that I did not have the courage to challenge the spider in her home territory, I knew I would somehow have to find the other outhouse—and soon—because my need was growing stronger with every passing second.

Back I went, seeking another fork that I thought would lead me to the other one. Abruptly I found myself confronting the outdoor shower stall and managed to grasp that it was not what I wanted. However, I knew that the other pit toilet was nearby and went off in search of it. Finally I spied it in the distance and with a great rush proceeded to it only to find that another enormous spider, a hairy black tarantula, was squatting in the exact same position as the first one. Horrified and confused, I looked to see whether I had simply doubled back and ended up at the same one again. After getting my bearings I understood that this indeed was the other outhouse and that yes, there were two giant spiders. Now I had no choice. I forced myself to approach the spider and it lowered itself in preparation to spring. Mercifully, it sprang toward a shadowy hole under the door of the stall. I rushed across just in time to take care of business. There was no relaxing, however, because in my mind the entire structure was filled with tarantulas. I scanned every nook and cranny of it, all the time realizing that at least one spider was lurking in that hole under the entrance only a couple of feet away.

As soon as I could, I exited that place and began my trek back to the ceremonial hut, but somehow I got off the path and ended up hopelessly lost among the plants of the botanical gardens. After a while I despaired of ever finding my way back. I was totally, helplessly lost even though the gardens were no bigger than an acre. Thankfully, I saw a beam of light and a voice inquired as to where I was. It was one of Pierre's assistants, whose job it was to bring back lost participants like me. He led me back by the arm, and when I saw the ceremonial hut, a place that it seemed I had not seen in many years, I breathed a huge sigh of relief.

As I lay back down in my spot, I began to have an extraordinary set of visions. I saw a kind of temple in front of me and I felt drawn to go and enter it. As I approached it I saw that it was filled with people who were bathed in the most extraordinary light coming from somewhere above them. I tried to enter the temple but it was so full of people, with their arms reaching above their heads receiving the light, that I could not get in. I had such a compelling desire to experience the light myself that I squeezed in, but I could only get the right side of my body into the temple and the light. The exquisite light, a kind of golden pink bluish color, penetrated my body, and I have never before experienced such bliss, such joy, even though I could not fully enter. It was like manna from heaven, the light of the Christ-force, the mighty I Am presence, and the rainbow light of the Buddhists.

I don't know how long this went on, but in a way the experience changed my life forever because now I knew what it was like to experience pure essence, with nothing left of my lower personality. There was nothing I wanted more than to remain in this light forever. Yet the vision gradually faded as the medicine wore off, and I felt both elated that I had felt such joy and loss at its leaving. I have never forgotten how this felt and how much I want to feel it again. I have no doubt I will when the time is right. It was a taste—a tempting taste of Spirit just to lure me on the spiritual path—but it was not enough to let me lose my focus on what I have to do here in the world.

It was also of note that it was only my right side, my masculine side, that I could get into the light. Perhaps my feminine side did not need to be healed in the same way. Time will tell, as it always does.

After the effects of the ayahuasca wore off in the early morning, I went out and sat with Carlos under a huge tree filled with the magic of thousands of fireflies, and we marveled at them together. Practically speechless, Carlos managed to mumble, with awe in his voice, "Dad, how do you manage to do this more than once?" With that comment I knew that his first experience with altered states had been awe inspiring and not something he would ever take lightly. We talked for hours, and I felt a new bond with him now that we had a mutual experience of something so powerful. He was now demonstrating an inquiring and insightful mind made sharper by his new experience. His days of just grunting at me were over. Many years later, he still considers it one of his most formative experiences, leading him on to a great many adventures of his own. He calls it a primary inspiration in his work as an animation director and producer.

Later my old friend Ron, the wildlife expert, joined us and waxed philosophical about what he had experienced. We had met in the first grade and now were sitting in the jungle in Peru so many years later sharing our thoughts and feelings. A great feeling of love seemed to envelop all of us as we watched the sky turn pink with the sunrise.

That day I sat talking with Pierre and he explained about jungle diets and how he was building a distant, more isolated compound in the deep jungle for doing such diets in great privacy and seclusion. From the minute he mentioned this, I knew it was something I wanted to do, yet it would be a private experience because I thought not many people would be willing to accompany me on such an adventure. How wrong I turned out to be! It was not too long before I found myself in Peru again for that very experience.

POSTSCRIPT

Sometimes we have to get lost to find ourselves. Even when we are lost, there are certain signs and symbols waiting to teach us something valuable.

Light is a shaman's best friend. Always look to the light for essence food. Sometimes we need to navigate darkness in order to reach the light of truth. That seems to be part of our process as human beings.

Even *part* of something good can be great. The desire for perfection and wholeness can sometimes get in the way of appreciating what is in the moment.

Sometimes we need to purge something in order to feel liberated. That purging can take place in many ways: energetically, symbolically, or by vomiting or shitting. Whichever way it comes out, the important thing is that it comes out to make room for more essence, more wisdom, more beauty, more love.

Another lesson learned: a structured and supervised experience with medicine in the right context can be a good one for young people—better than having one on the urban streets.

QUESTIONS

Have you ever had a dream or a vision that was so compelling, so real that it felt life-changing? How did it impact your life? What did it show you about what you needed? Do you allow yourself to have higher-centered experiences on a regular basis? Do you let these experiences transform you or do you write them off as just strange?

8

THE POWER OF DIETING IN THE JUNGLE

Plant Teachings

Six months after our visit to Pierre's compound, in April 1997, I was returning to Peru, accompanied by my friend Richard, a Peruvian-born clinical psychologist-hypnotherapist living and working in the Santa Fe region. We had arranged with Pierre to travel to his new, isolated compound deep in the jungle to diet for greater knowledge of the teacher plant ayahuasca. We were thrilled at the prospect, and appreciating Pierre's vast knowledge of the plants, we were somewhat anxious about what we would encounter. Pierre had supervised many diets and warned us about the intensity of dieting and that it could produce profound results; it was not to be taken lightly. En route to Peru, both Richard and I experienced powerful dreams about transformation in the depths of the jungle. Somehow we knew this journey would change our lives irrevocably. It was not every day that we could spend time in ceremony with a master ayahuasqero.

After a brief stay in his compound, we readied for the journey to *la selva profunda*, a place called Regalia in the deep jungle, where we would continue the diet and seek plant knowledge. Pierre wanted us to have the experience of being away from all civilization, in virgin jungle where the plant spirits would be most powerful.

In the night prior to leaving, I was seized by cramping, diarrhea, and vomiting, probably the result of some bad airport food—not an auspicious way to begin such a difficult trip to the wilds of the Amazon, but I had come too far to be deterred. Pierre prepared a plant concoction for me that soothed the cramping and settled my stomach. Without further delay, we piled into two dusty taxis with bald tires for the wild overland part of the journey. Richard and I were accompanied by Arturo Benitez, a Cuban-born student of teacher plants in his seventies; Ernesto, a young Peruvian; forty-five-year-old Miguel Rostas, an assistant and apprentice shaman to Pierre; and of course Pierre himself, under whose direction we would be working. This would be the first group of four to work at the new site. With time and hard work, Pierre would eventually be able to take up to twelve guests who wished to diet under his supervision.

On the way, both taxis suffered the obligatory flat tire and repair, making the trip a long one. According to Pierre, journeys such as these always include tests and obstacles to overcome, and even certain sacrifices. The sacrifice had begun.

Eventually we arrived at a large river that ultimately joins the Amazon. Here we were required to show passports to grim, machine gun–toting Peruvian Marines who have established a base and checkpoint to combat traffic in coca, the principle plant ingredient in the manufacture of cocaine. We breathed a deep sigh of relief when all our documents checked out and we were allowed to pass. We learned from Pierre that many of the local people had abandoned their coca fields and were turning to other ways to make a living. He had hired some of them himself to help build his jungle compound.

At this checkpoint we left the taxis behind and transferred to a long, narrow, open-air motorboat for a two-hour journey through breathtaking, pristine jungle, accompanied by flying parakeets, kingfishers, egrets, and all manner of other birds. We passed homesteads and villages slashed out of the forest, their palm frond–thatched roofs sheltering the natives from the torrential downpours that inundate the Amazon basin at all times of the year.

Upon reaching a smaller tributary with deep green waters, we transferred to a small dugout that carried us for another hour to the take-out where we would begin our walking trek to the small compound an hour away. Weakened from my bout with illness, I was fortunate to have help carrying my pack through dense forest darkened further by dusk, which, at the equator, arrives at six o'clock sharp. We were joined by Julio Tigre, a local and knowledgeable hunter, and by Humberto, who would be our cook. The diet requires that for men, the cook be a young boy or an older man who is no longer actively sexual, lest the food preparation be compromised or influenced by energies not focused on the plant medicines. Kindly Humberto, appearing to be in his late fifties, was this man.

Finally, we arrived at the mouth of a small river with a trail leading into the jungle. Sweating, panting, and whacking our way through the Peruvian jungle with machetes, our group of eight slowly made its way to the compound on the banks of the beautiful Rio Respata.

The trek led us up over a ridge through a dense forest with massive trees hung with vines and thick shrubs. The vines were so thick that they themselves could be classified as tree trunks. At one point I brushed past a large leaf and discovered that fierce, biting ants had spilled down my shirt and had instantly begun biting my flesh. I realized in a flash that the jungle was intensely alive and that I must be vigilant. A few minutes later my resolve was strengthened when we stumbled upon a coiled rattlesnake, a fer-de-lance (iron spear), one of the deadliest poisonous snakes in the world. The jungle would not be easy. Breaking out of the deep forest, we arrived at the compound to the roar of an exquisite waterfall forty feet across on the Rio Respata.

After much exploring, Pierre had found this pristine location, a place untouched by human beings, where the plant and animal spirits are active and strong. Here there had been no logging, no road building, and no human activity, and there would be no intrusion of human sounds or thoughts. During the diet it is imperative not to be interrupted by strangers because their sudden presence could spoil its positive effects. One must be relatively quiet and in a private place or the effects of the plants could become twisted and cause harm rather than good.

Here we would remain for the duration of the diet: meditating; doing ceremony; studying the plants; and bathing in the juices of their bark, flowers, leaves, and stems. There was an open-sided shelter about fifteen feet long with a palm frond roof for sleeping under mosquito netting and holding ceremony, a small cookhouse for dining, and another small shelter for staff sleeping quarters. All around the shelters, the jungle towered into the sky, its deep green a contrast to the brilliant blue of the equatorial sky surrounding the always-forming clouds.

In the Amazon, night falls rapidly, and after arranging our gear and setting up the sleeping pads, we drifted indoors to enjoy a delicious light supper and meet some of our new companions. After dinner we learned more about which plants each of us would ingest and diet with. As I mentioned before, Richard and I would be concentrating on the plant combination called ayahuasca. The ayahuasca vine is combined with the leaves of a small tree called *chacruna*. The leaves of the chacruna tree contribute the visionary DMT (dimethyltryptamine), and the ayahuasca vine contains harmaline, an MAO inhibitor. The combination produces the deeply sacred healing experience referred to only as "taking ayahuasca." Ernesto was going to focus on albahaca, the basil plant, for cleansing and purification, while Arturo was choosing to take chiric sanango root for physical strength and endurance. On previous trips to Peru, Arturo had worked with several other plants to great advantage. He described a diet he had taken several years earlier with *ushpa-washa sanango*, a plant that for a week helped him remember in great detail and order all the significant memories of his life starting in childhood. He described a kind of detachment he felt as he saw the interrelationship of all his life's events and how together they had contributed to who he had become. He found this experience very valuable.

During this new diet over the next several days, Arturo would shiver with cold from the effects of chiric sanango. The shivering produced by the plant is a manifestation of its properties. Even its name in Quechua, the language of the Incas, means "cold." This plant is often taken to get rid of cold or damp conditions in the body, such as rheumatism. The shivering is a way of releasing the cold from the body. People often think of the Amazon as hot, but it is possible to suffer from hypothermia because of the dampness, frequent travel on rivers, and the occasional cold winds from the south. Arthritis and rheumatism are big problems in the Amazon and chiric sanango is a great blessing to the people.

For Richard and me, the diet dictated by Pierre consisted of the following: for two weeks prior to the intensive deep jungle experience, we avoided medications, chilies, pork, iced or very cold drinks, acidic foods like vinegar, strong spices, alcohol, lard, and sex, including erotic fantasy. We were to spend time quietly preparing ourselves for the inner work and avoid a hectic lifestyle that might include disturbing articles, television programs, or films, and even attending conferences. As I later learned from Miguel, this is a classic diet used for many plants in the Amazon, the main point of which is to allow the body to build up strength for the rigors of the diet in the jungle. Avoiding sex and a hectic lifestyle is designed to stop energy leaks so energy can build up in preparation for the ingestion of the plant.

The "diet," of course, is much more than food restrictions. According to Pierre, it is inclusive of many things: one is to rest and avoid worry, distractions, and intense feelings. The diet is for purification, clearing, and making oneself open and available to the teachings of the plants. Anything that shocks the body is to be avoided.

After we arrived at the compound in the deep jungle, the diet continued in earnest, with an even more rigorous schedule. We were allowed to eat the flesh of the *boqui chico*, an Amazon River fish whose flesh is considered pure because it eats only fruit. These fish are rather bony and small but nonetheless delicious when cooked. With the fish we could eat cooked plain plantains, something like a banana but less tasty and somewhat chalky when prepared over a fire. On occasion we could eat plain white rice, and near the latter part of the diet we dined on *paca*, a large, tasty rodent with dark meat that lives in the jungle, and on a pheasantlike bird that tasted somewhat like chicken. We ate these foods twice, sometimes three times a day. The meals were never filling and completely without spice, but we relished them all the same.

We were to avoid a lot of talk, joking, and distracting activity in order to concentrate on the plant teachings. We were to benefit from the powerful spiritual influence of the forest and avoid non-dieting human beings with other agendas who could disturb the diet with their strong emotions. Since we were all focused on a single theme, we did not need to be isolated from one another, but we maintained minimal contact except at mealtimes.

Pierre warned us that many things could interrupt the diet and even ruin it, such as interference from an animal we might encounter. We were told that if we should suddenly meet an animal in the jungle, we should never joke about it or laugh at it but rather show it utmost respect. In this way, the animal would not disturb the diet and might even help with it.

Each day we were to consume some of the plant, either in raw form or specially cooked and prepared. The ayahuasca vine is ceremonially cut into foot-long sections, stripped of bark, pounded to a pulp, and layered alternately in a large pot with leaves from the chacruna plant (and sometimes other plants from other parts of the Amazon) and is then cooked over a low flame for six to ten or more hours. I learned that each shaman prepares the medicine according to a slightly different recipe based on his or her own understanding with the plant. The juice is further boiled down to form a concentrate. Throughout the cooking process, according to tradition, the shaman prays into the plant using tobacco smoke to assure that it is honored and will be helpful to those who consume it. Before the concentrate is consumed, Pierre, like all Amazonian shamans, prays and sends the prayers via tobacco smoke into the bottle of concentrated medicine. The medicine is then consumed in the form of a tea, usually in rather small amounts (about a shot glass).

On the two non-ceremony evenings, we ingested a teaspoon of ayahuasca to maintain its presence in our bodies. The effect was vivid, lucid dreams during the night. On the five ceremony nights we ingested from thirty to forty milliliters of reconstituted ayahuasca in a small ceramic cup—about an ounce to an ounce and a third.

Pierre told us that each preparation is different in concentration and potency and has to be experimented with to find the proper dosage to produce the visions and healing affects. He also explained the different varieties of the ayahuasca vine and how each can have a distinct strength and effect. In Peru, the vine comes in a common yellow variety, a rare white-fleshed one that grows in the highlands, and a black vine that is very strong and more delicate to work with. This black variety is considered to have much magic but its diet is very strict. According to Pierre, few shamans are willing to diet so rigorously, restricting themselves to eating one variety of fish for every meal for their whole lives, for example. The yellow vine is lower in potency but easily found and therefore used in most ceremonies. This is the variety we worked with during our diet. The vine itself can grow thick like a tree, but for ceremonial purposes it is used when it is about one and a half to two inches in diameter, after five years of growth.

The days were given to rest, integration, and preparation for the evening ceremonies. After a day of lounging and napping in the hammocks slung between the trunks of tall trees laden with green vines, or floating in the freshwater pool below the tumbling cool waterfall, we gathered in the dusk to bathe in water suffused with various plants stems, leaves, and flowers. Some of these plants included *guayusa* (a plant that gives strength), *ajo sacha*, *luasha*, and *chiric sanango*, all plants with purifying qualities. Their purpose was to cleanse both our physical and spirit bodies before ingesting the diet plant.

After bathing and air drying, we entered the shelter for the ayahuasca ceremony. Since, according to Pierre, light is considered incompatible with ayahuasca, all ceremonies took place in total darkness, without even a candle for light. Without a moon the jungle becomes pitch black at night until the plant reveals the intrinsic light within the structure of the whole environment. Then the jungle lights up with the luminescence of its own magic. Trees and plants glow with their own iridescence, fireflies flit by the thousands in the branches of the overhanging trees, and each human emits a colorful energetic radiance almost impossible to describe in its ephemeral complexity and beauty.

To consume ayahuasca while safe at home in an enclosed room in your own culture is one thing. To partake of it in the intensity of the deep jungle with giant insects buzzing, spiders crawling, frogs and toads croaking, snakes slithering, birds singing, and a host of mammals of the jungle snorting and screaming in the night is quite another. People think the deep jungle is quiet, but nothing could be further from the truth. It is as noisy as a carnival. Not only is it thick with the noise of wildlife, but it is the home of countless plant and animal spirits waiting to reveal their secrets to the shamanic seeker.

During the first ceremony the spirit of a large vulture I had seen during the day taught me about forgiveness and told me not to be so hard on myself. During another ceremony a huge snake spirit slithered into my mouth and through my intestines, cleaning me out in the most personal and thorough way. A great green frog warned me about negative thoughts, and the felt presence of a screaming monkey out in the dark invited me to stay focused and pay attention.

Needless to say, the dark, deep forest can raise your terror level to a high degree. This is one of the personal confrontations that the diet offers: a chance to face nameless fear and overcome it. I was soon to discover that it was not the jungle that I was afraid of. The fear was within me, and I had brought it with me to the jungle.

Those of us focusing on the ayahuasca diet, as well as several others in the group, partook of the tea in a sacred manner like a communion and then settled down on our pads to wait for the teachings and visions from within. The ceremonies are indescribable, and no words can ever capture the true nature of the event. All the senses are involved: the bitter taste of the tea; the sounds of the jungle and the icaros of the shamans; the acrid smell of tobacco and the sweetness of Agua Florida; the touch of the shaman's ministrations and the prickly heat of the night; and the intense inner visions of patterns, landscapes, and animals. Never have I experienced such feelings of mortality as in the jungle. Never have I received such clarity of wisdom, such teachings, such awareness as in this series of ceremonies. Never have I been consumed with such trepidation, such elation, and such challenges as in this diet.

During the evening sessions, the guiding shamans, Pierre and Miguel, donned their sacred robes decorated with Shipibo designs, sang the icaros, guided the medicine, and shaped the visions. In turns they worked with us, blew on us, sang over us, and healed us. After many hours we clustered in the darkness to share our visions and newly gained knowledge. Seldom have I felt such love, such camaraderie, such a sense of belonging and rightness in the work we were doing together.

As we gathered for the first ceremony I was elated about where I was and what was about to take place. My need for adventure was more than completely satisfied, especially when a snake fell from the roof of the hut and landed among us, rising up and weaving back and forth like a cobra. We all scrambled to get away until the cook identified it as nonpoisonous and took it out to the forest on a stick. It occurred to me that such omens are not accidental, and I prepared for a powerful journey into the world of ayahuasca. The medicine, a dark brown viscous liquid, had been prepared in Iquitos and was now stored in several clear liter bottles.

We arranged ourselves in a circle around Pierre and watched as he lit a pipe and blew the smoke many times into a bottle of ayahuasca. Then one by one, we crawled to sit in front of him as he measured out a small portion for us to drink. The taste of ayahuasca can vary a great deal and this time it was quite sweet, with a bitter aftertaste. After ingesting and mentally asking the medicine to help me "see," I crawled back to my spot to await the visions. In a surprisingly short time, about twenty minutes, I began to feel its effects. I had a sense of disequilibrium and imbalance, with a quickening of images behind closed eyes. When the visions began in earnest, I felt it necessary to lie back and I hardly budged for the next several hours. Ayahuasca carries the nickname of "the little death" for this reason. The activity is all internal and the body can be as still as a corpse.

Early in this first ceremony of the diet, I experienced a great deal of fear. I worried about spiders and bugs crawling on me, and certainly the mosquitoes were out and about. Perhaps I had bitten off more than I could chew, I thought, and I had to draw on some of my skills as a therapist to calm myself down. After a while Pierre sang delightful icaros in a falsetto voice and the effect on me was profound. Later he told me that the first icaros are to call the spirit of ayahuasca and other protective spirits, declare our good intentions and goodwill, and set up a structure for optimal conditions. Later the icaros would relate to each participant in turn—focusing on learning, healing, supporting, giving strength, and the like.

When the first icaros began, about an hour after we had ingested, I was experiencing the jungle's power and its many presences, and I felt befriended by the spirit of ayahuasca. Its spirit appeared to me as a beautiful if not seductive woman who could teach me about my feminine nature. She danced in a writhing fashion and spoke directly to me as she transformed into a stunning green snake and then into vines, curving and coiling. She taught me that it is the nature of the feminine to curve and have rounded edges and that I could benefit from learning to be less linear and discover my curves as well. I listened and watched and asked her to teach me more.

After a time, Pierre called my name and I crawled to sit in front of him where he asked me how I was doing. I could hardly sit up, much less talk, so he blew tobacco smoke over me and sang icaros. Later he told me that he was asking the spirit of various places of power to enter me to help me on my journey within the jungle. He also sang to the spirit of ayahuasca to help me to learn and see as much as possible. He moved his hands over and around my energy field, healing and creating balance where before there had been rifts and disharmonies. Eventually he blew smoke into the top of my head and into my hands, which he folded in prayer fashion within his own hands. He finished off with Agua Florida, which he blew over me for cleansing and spread on my forehead, under my ears, and on my hands to open up the energy centers there. As he did all this the visions increased immeasurably in their intensity and power. I thanked him and then he handed me over to Miguel, who ministered to me with his own icaros. After probably forty-five minutes I crawled back to my spot. This would be the structure for the four following ceremonies as well. The icaros they sang each evening and the places where they concentrated their healing changed every time. I estimated that they spent about forty-five minutes with each of us, and clearly they worked very hard without ceasing until the ceremony ended.

Occasionally their songs were obscured by the sound of someone vomiting over the side of the hut into the jungle. Being a purgative, ayahuasca often makes people throw up or have a bowel movement. Pierre told us not to resist if the ayahuasca wished to cleanse our bodies. Although I did not feel the need the first night of ceremony, I experienced the purgative effect on subsequent nights. I noticed that the nausea resulting in vomiting was always accompanied by disharmonious thoughts. I realized that ayahuasca was also helping rid our systems of psychological baggage.

Many other visions accompanied this first ceremony, and by about two in the morning I felt a lessening of the plant's intensity. Then Pierre called us together to have us give our renditions of the main experiences of the evening. My Spanish-language skills being only fair, I struggled to understand the words, but somehow the teachings and the sharing communicated to me anyway. Perhaps it was best that I could not follow every word. Around three in the morning we lay down to sleep—that is, if we could. I could not, so I just rested until dawn. If I was lucky, I would nap in the hammock before the next night. I found going without sleep was an important part of the experience because it allowed me to be more in touch with my vulnerabilities and the areas that needed exorcising in my subconscious. After several days of dieting, ceremony, and little sleep, I found myself very emotional and in touch with the hurt child deep inside me.

During the second ceremony I experienced a flood of tears for that inner child who had endured so much loneliness and abandonment when I was very young. I grew up as a latchkey child because both my parents worked from the time I was about four years old. I saw this part of myself in a kind of transparency that I had never been able to reach through years of psycho-therapy and intensive growth experiences. I saw with clarity the workings of the ego I had developed to cope with hardship, my feeble attempts to defend myself from an abusive older brother, my silly self-deception that I was special somehow, and my limi-tations regarding self-confidence and social skills, and I saw the source of a great inner strength lying behind all the garbage. I realized how dictatorial my inner demands for perfection had been and saw the actuality of my imperfections just as they were. The ayahuasca spirit showed me objectively and neutrally where I lacked discipline and how my fear prevented me from taking advantage of opportunities that had come my way. I saw my humanity and the blend of my essence as it works through me, and I saw much more. This second ceremony was a major purge and left me in a deeply relaxed and accepting state.

As I mentioned earlier, we drank a little ayahuasca on alter-nate nights to keep it active in our systems throughout our sleep without actually doing a major ceremony. These nights were filled with lucid dreams of a highly valuable nature. I dreamed I was taken to faraway inner landscapes that I recognized as places I visited in my childhood daydreams. Spirit beings that I remembered as old friends showed me that I had always been connected beneath the surface, even during the trying and lonely years of my early childhood. They now gave me instructions about what I needed to do to change my life for the better. They showed me that gratitude is the key to having whatever I seek in my life. They also reminded me how important it is for me to communicate my love and concern to my children, my wife, and the other people who truly matter to me.

During the third ceremony I had an exceptionally difficult experience. After ingesting the tea from the same bottle as the nights before and taking the same amount, I experienced total overwhelm. The visions came stronger and stronger until I felt that I had been pushed to my limit and could go no further, but still the intensity kept building. I felt as if I had risen to a great height and was being pushed against a ceiling with tremendous force. I was not able to penetrate it and felt stuck there, with fear growing in me every second. During this time, I became aware that Pierre was repeatedly throwing up and was not yet available to help me. Miguel was occupied by singing some icaros to help him. Later they explained to me that they sometimes needed to do some healing work on each other before they could focus on healing others.

Finally, feeling panic setting in, I crawled over to Pierre and told him I felt the medicine's effects were too strong and I was having trouble with fear. He asked me laconically what I meant by "too strong" and I couldn't answer his question. Later he told me that it was only "too strong" in my belief and that I was dealing with a self-imposed limitation. I was to discover a rich vein of understanding in his words when I pondered them afterward.

At the time he began to sing an icaro to the medicine, and after a short while I felt the intensity of the ayahuasca diminish to the point where I could manage it. I felt great respect for his ability to talk to the medicine and get it to do his bidding. I now knew what he meant when he said that dieting without a shaman is very risky and not a good idea.

I felt relief beyond measure and then received positive and informative words of wisdom from the plant spirit. The ayahuasca showed me how to gather up energy from my surroundings wherever I happened to be—a forest, the seashore, the mountains, the desert. The spirit of the plant warned me that I should ask the environment for protection on a forthcoming rafting trip through the Grand Canyon. It showed me how foolish it was to take such a journey without asking the spirit of the terrain for permission to trespass and request safe passage. I thought of all the times I had taken risks and neglected to take this precaution. I vowed to mend my ways, and the subsequent three-week trip down the Colorado River was injury- and illness-free for all the participants.

During the fourth ceremony I consumed the same dosage of medicine that I had on prior nights but I experienced very little effect. After about two hours I told Pierre and he gave me an additional dose of the tea and did healing work with me. This slightly increased the effect, but throughout the rest of the evening I felt disappointment that I had not reached the levels of visions and insight of previous evenings. I felt a great deal of emotional pain upon listening to the powerful experiences of the others at the end of the evening, knowing that I had lost a special opportunity.

At that time I asked Pierre why I experienced so little, even with an extra dosage. He explained that fear and resistance could completely block the effect of the ayahuasca and that it had to do with my intense fear experience from the night before. I found this phenomenon most interesting food for thought because it showed me the power of my mind in relation to the effects of the plant. I could clearly see what Pierre was getting at when he had asked me what I meant by the medicine being "too strong" the other evening. Obviously the intensity level was quite clearly under my control. I felt it was too much one night and with an even stronger dosage I felt it was not enough the next night. Pierre went on to explain that ayahuasca is finicky and very sensitive. If it does not feel welcome it won't show up, even with very high dosages.

During the fifth ceremony, I was convinced I was not going to make it out of the jungle alive. I was losing weight, I was dehydrated, and my body was covered with insect bites. During this final ingestion of ayahuasca I saw and experienced vivid visions of my emaciated body on a tattered sixteenth-century sailing vessel strewn with the bodies of starving and dying sailors. I lost all contact with the jungle and truly thought I was on that ship. The winds were listless, the sails sagging and lifeless, the ship in a state of disarray and decay. I fought the image, I battled against imminent death, I resisted with what was left of my flagging energy. I felt a great sadness that I would never see my family again or my home and my dog. Then, after what seemed like a long time, I came to a place of peace. Yes, perhaps I would die on this vessel with the others and it was okay. I had the realization that to die is actually to wake up from a dream and be born into a nonphysical reality, and that being born into this physical body is to fall asleep in that other reality. I understood that this process was completely natural and happened in an infinite cycle until all was in balance and harmony. I saw that when an animal or plant dies, it wakes up and says, "Oh, I have been dreaming that I was a tree, a blade of grass, a butterfly, a bird, a fox, a snake, or a buffalo." Then it eventually falls asleep again and dreams once more that it is living in the forest as an animal or a plant. Although I had always known this intellectually, I now knew it experientially at the core level of truth. I understood on a deeper level now why ayahuasca has the nickname "the little death"; it is not only to lie very still but also to know death and yet live a while longer, the wiser for it.

I was given many other teachings during this powerful culminating ceremony. I saw that Mother Earth gives to her children freely so we may eat and stay alive, and that we must never forget where our food comes from and give thanks for this great gift. I was shown indescribable visions of beauty and wondrous landscapes containing the most exquisite plant and animal forms, and I was shown that this beauty exists always within all things. I experienced a profound sense of gratitude for my life, for the incredible good fortune of being created and having the opportunity to experience this grand adventure. And I remembered how as a child sitting in church, bored with the service, I'd had these very feelings—before I became an adult and forgot. These were just a few of the many gifts of the plant spirit after the issue of death had been resolved.

Eventually the spirit of my dog showed up to check on me and provide me some solace. I cried with tears of gratitude for her love, comfort, and company.

In the morning of the eighth day I awoke weak but very much alive. I didn't think I would get through it but I did. We had fish soup to break our strict diet—never did a thin, salty soup taste so good. We packed and hiked out to meet our boat for the return trip home, bitten, thinner, weaker, and much wiser.

The diet, however, was not over. For two weeks afterward we were required to follow the same regime as before our arrival. The intense dreams continued for the entire duration of the diet, even days after we left the jungle.

In a shamanic sense, the diet is highly effective in fulfilling its intended purpose: to cleanse us in preparation for accepting the plant ally and the power it brings. First we were plucked away from everything familiar: the city, friends, foods, entertainment, and work. We were plunked down into an alien environment, the selva profunda, a spectacular, gorgeous, dangerous situation where we depended entirely on those who knew how to survive there. We were given a strict diet under the guidance of experienced shamans and were asked to remain silent, with much of the day given to self-reflection and introspection.

Little by little the false self broke down. The intellect had little to do and emotions rose to the surface. Sadness, fears, angers, and limitations revealed themselves to be purged. Childhood patterns and memories became clear and tears flowed in a flood of release. After five days of intense plant journeys in this powerful jungle environment, I had begun to let go. I sobbed out my old sadness, my childhood wounds. I cried about how I had allowed fear to run me for so long. I have already described how I reflected upon my isolation and alienation growing up and how even now, as an adult, connection with others can be so difficult. The teacher plant showed me, at times harshly, at times gently, who I am. I saw my self-pity, my resistance, and my lack of resolve in the face of hardship. I was able to see the fear of death and loss that had hounded me and blocked joy, elation, and peace.

Great weight lifted from my chest. I gave these sorrows to the jungle and prayed for healing, an open heart, strength, and direction. I felt the love of my family, and I knew without a doubt that I was loved and I could love myself. I experienced a most profound healing and a new sense of the power that comes from recognizing the essence self. I also recognized how much work I had yet to do if I was to fulfill my true potential in this life.

Upon my return to the United States, even after so short a trip, I experienced some culture shock and a need for adjustment. I was profoundly tired and slept for two entire days and nights with little break. My insect bites required attention, and I ate voraciously to gain back the weight I had lost. When I returned to work as a consultant, counselor, and writer, I was gratified to discover a new sense of clarity and focus. I experienced more humility and patience toward myself and others. I found myself kinder and more compassionate, yet less tolerant of self-pity and distraction. I felt a greater depth of affection and appreciation for my family and a sense of confidence and power that I had not known before.

In this encounter with the power of the jungle a part of me died and another part was born. Comparing notes on the way home I discovered that this was also the case for my companion Richard, with whom a new bond was forged. Bear in mind that not everyone will have an experience exactly like ours; it may be much easier or much more difficult. Many should perhaps never attempt the diet at all because the experience is rigorous and clearly not for everyone. One has to be physically strong and emotionally prepared for such a challenge. Otherwise the diet can simply be overwhelming or too hard on the body. Those who have the interest, the tenacity, the time, and the means may receive great gifts from the challenge of dieting with the plants in the jungle.

I do not wish to misrepresent or overstate my experience with plant dieting in any way. According to Pierre and other shamans we met, the diet we pursued was minimal. Even though we prepared for two weeks prior and followed up for two weeks after, a week is quite brief as diets go and often they are much longer—fifteen days or even a month or more. Some diets may take over a year to fulfill. Ours was a beginner's diet that allowed some abilities to work with the plant as an ally. For greater depth, a longer diet is necessary.

Pierre, Miguel, and other knowledgeable shamans like them follow a courageous discipline, healing the sick, working with the plants, and helping preserve the tradition and great wisdom of the teacher plants. Not only is this knowledge endangered by today's world, but Pierre told me that many shamans today are losing their way to corruption and the enticements of modern life. Fast money, alcoholism, power, and the seduction of sex with those Northerners who are easily seduced by the charms of the mystical Latin shamans derail more than a few.

Thankfully there are still shamans with integrity who can be trusted to teach, show, and heal with love and dedication. Pierre is one. His vision includes documenting the healing properties of many jungle plants; keeping track of the ancient recipes for their preparation; creating diets and plant combinations that have major healing potential for such diseases as cancer, tuberculosis, AIDS, depression, and a host of other maladies; creating a context for people to diet in the proper manner to gain knowledge of the teacher plants; and practicing shamanism in the traditional ways for healing and balance.

POSTSCRIPT

Ceremonies can be like structured emergencies, ritualized dramas that present all manner of emotionally charged situations for healing and integration. They happen in the safety of a supervised setting in response to a powerful medicine and are confined by the time limits of the medicine, not unlike the structure of a longish psychotherapy session. In this case the medicine is the psychotherapist. Much can be learned from a structured and planned mini-psychosis. Experiences of the psyche are reframed and shuffled into a different and more productive configuration.

Here are some of the lessons I learned from my experience with the teacher plant ayahuasca:

- Be grateful without taking anything for granted. Say hello to every little thing and it will say hello back. In this way the world wakes up.

- Amazing beauty is embedded everywhere; it's just overlooked at times. Sometimes an altered state will help reveal that beauty that has hidden behind everyday perception and busyness.

- It is good to question automatic beliefs and reactions. They may have limitations that can be lifted for greater access to power.

- Never underestimate the power of a diet. Real diets may include not just types of food, but dieting from certain types of thoughts, behaviors, addictions, experiences, and ways of perceiving that are limiting.

- Support is all around us. Our animal friends are with us even when they are not physically present.

- Surrendering can be the most productive course of action on the road to power.

EXERCISE

Dieting can be associated with anything. You may diet with food, plants, thoughts, or experiences. Choose something that you are going to do without for a brief period of time (from three to ten days). It may be a tendency toward certain ways of thinking, or drinking coffee, having yogurt or ice cream, drinking sodas, driving your car, watching TV, or hanging out with certain persons. Change it up for a few days. Break up your schedule, do things you have never done before, change your sleep patterns, or what have you. Experience a shift in the routine and observe what happens. What happens when you don't have your regularly scheduled lunch or dinner? How do you react? What comes up to take its place? What feelings come up inside of you?

9

THE POWER OF COMMUNION

A Magical Andes Wedding

———————————————

As usual, the list of travelers for our seventeen-day trip through the Peruvian Andes changed many times prior to our departure as various people signed on and then dropped away and others on the waiting list took their place. Nevertheless, although we did not consciously plan it, we ended up with exactly the perfect group: twelve men and twelve women, eight couples, thirteen Canadians, ten Americans, Lena and me, and one Australian. And what a wonderful mix we were!

The trip began in Lima, and our first destination was Cusco (Qosqo), the place the Peruvians call the navel of the world. We acclimated to the eleven-thousand-foot altitude and enjoyed the town's colonial ambiance while visiting the powerful local temples. We saw the uniting of the Condor and the Eagle, the ancient prophecy about the eventual meeting of North and South America, documented in pre-Incan carvings of the stone temples. The next part of our journey took us through the Sacred Valley of the Incas to Pisac, the Temple of the Condor, Ollantaytambo, and the Temple of the Lama and the Earth. Early in the trip we prepared a despacho, an offering representing each of us that we would take along and finally burn on the Island of Amantani in Lake Titicaca. The stage was set for understanding the important Incan relationships among the condor of the upper world, the jaguar of the middle world, and the serpent of the lower world, representing truth, love, and energy, respectively, the three building blocks of the universe. With our guide Puma's assistance, we clearly saw the vision and power of prophecy of the pre-Incan seers and the extraordinary understanding with which they approached their world.

At Machu Picchu, a Canadian couple, Tony and Susan, decided to get married and asked me to perform the ceremony, which I gladly did. That is another wonderful story all its own. However, the tale I want to focus on comes when we traveled to Lake Titicaca.

After the group arrived in Puno on the shores of the lake, two of our members became ill, so we arranged for them to stay behind in the hotel while the rest of us traveled to Amantani by boat. On the way there, a most extraordinary event took place. By this time we had come to realize that this was no ordinary trip to the Andes. While I was down below in the boat explaining the *chacana*, the Andean cross, to some of our travelers, Lena and others in our group were on the roof of the boat when they saw fire in the sky. It looked like something was falling into the lake, trailing rainbow-colored flames behind it. No one knew what it was just then, but it was big; it could have been a rocket, a piece of a space station, or a meteor. On the island, all the inhabitants were talking about it. Several days later we discovered that it had indeed been a meteor that hit the ground near the shores of the lake, creating a crater and causing an international incident. Apparently, the meteor punched a hole in the aquifer, which then gave off such malodorous odors that it caused many people and animals in the area to become ill.

We contemplated the odds that our group would see a meteor fall and hit the earth during the day. We also discussed Lake Titicaca as the new spiritual center for the planet, which had shifted from Tibet, a masculine center, to the lake, a feminine center in the world. For this reason, Tibetan lamas, including the Dalai Lama, had recently visited this area; they had been exchanging information and passing the baton to the Incan priests in the Andes. The Dalai Lama had also suggested that his next incarnation may be born in Peru, another sign that a shift had occurred, as the Dalai Lama is considered to be the same incarnated soul each time. It is believed that no prior Dalai Lama has ever been born outside Tibet. Now a very visible meteor lands next to the lake in full daylight. Most interesting.

On Amantani we did our ceremonial climb to the temples of the sun and moon on the twin peaks of the island, accompanied by many members of the families we stayed with, including a little band with flutes and a drum. The townspeople had dressed up Susan in traditional garb, so she took the hike in festive native attire. After visiting the temple of the sun, which was locked, as usual, we crossed the island to the temple of the moon, which to our amazement was open, though it had been closed on many prior visits. Our guide Gabriel, a local paqo, contemplated a moment and then, because it was open, invited us inside the circular temple. In we went to perform a ceremony.

We set up an altar and called in the eagle and the condor to preside, and as Lena began a beautiful song, a towering dust column formed just outside. Like a mini tornado, it jumped the wall of the temple and swirled among us, blinding everyone with blowing coca leaves, dust, and everything from the altar. I watched my vest sail a hundred feet into the air to disappear somewhere outside. Amazingly, Lena had the presence to continue singing as if nothing was happening, and suddenly the tornado was gone and all was calm. Everyone was stunned by this phenomenon. Gabriel said it was a most auspicious sign. So we put the altar together again and called up one of our travelers to honor her on her fiftieth birthday. After everyone hugged her, we called up the Canadians Tony and Susan to honor their relationship.

They had planned a wedding in November back home in Canada, but after witnessing their friends' wedding in Machu Picchu, they were so moved and inspired that they wanted to do some kind of ceremony for their own engagement on this trip. Tony had sidled up to me the night before and asked if we could do something on the mountain the next day. So we called them up to stand in front of everyone, Susan looking most beautiful in her native attire and Tony with a native scarf; they looked just like a local couple about to get married. Suddenly a local woman jumped to Susan's side and Gabriel jumped to Tony's side to be the maid of honor and best man, and all the local women and men jumped up because they saw that it was a wedding—or perhaps they just wanted it to be one.

We honored the couple and everyone cried, and our friends got exactly what they had asked for. Once again I performed a wedding in a most wonderful place. After everyone congratulated them, we filed out and, at thirteen thousand feet, had a big traditional dance in the field outside with the band playing and the fabulous blue Lake Titicaca shining in every direction. Then the townswomen prepared a big feast of tubers, potatoes, fish, corn, and beer that they had lugged up the mountain on their backs almost as if they knew there would be a grand celebration. We were all more than amazed, and everyone had to admit the trip was just getting better and better and better. It was possible to be happy day after day after day without the usual grumpiness and complaining that happens on long trips to foreign lands. In great joy, we danced our way down the mountain holding hands with our Andean hosts. Later they told us this was one of their most wonderful and powerful traditions.

After leaving the island we flew to Arequipa for the final leg of our journey: to Colca Canyon to witness the flight of the condors. We took a bus to Chivay, and on the way, crossing the pass at fifteen thousand feet, we got out to add our personal touch to the thousands of cairns left for good fortune over the years by countless travelers. We were surrounded by snow-covered peaks in every direction, mountains held sacred by the Incan people.

At Chivay, a wonderful mountain village, we visited beautiful hot springs and soaked away some travel weariness. Upon arriving at our hotel in a wonderful mountain village, we were greeted by villagers celebrating a fertility festival and were immediately drawn into dancing and music all over again. The hotel boasted views of all the major apus (sacred mountains) all around and we once again feasted.

The next morning saw us up early to catch the bus to witness the condors as they circled up the thermals to fly over the cliffs. This is an event that simply cannot be described adequately. The condors circled up by the dozens, so majestic, so full of power and grace, blessing everyone in the hushed crowd of observers from every nation. It is hard to explain how the flight of these birds can bring one to tears but my deepest emotions came to the surface. After the great birds had gone, we drove back to the village for rest and free time and that night celebrated yet again with a feast and music, singing, and much laughter. Yes, it's true: Canadians are a wild bunch, and all it takes is one additional Australian to make an outstanding party. Sprinkle in a few Americans to appreciate it all and to get a little permission to be bad, and voilà—you have the makings of a truly good time.

The next morning, now addicted to the grand birds, we decided to swing by and watch the condors again on our way back to Arequipa. We also spotted an eagle and several hawks, and some giant Andean hummingbirds balanced out the scene. This day the condors put on an even better display than the day before, spiraling and gliding around and around our heads and coming close enough that we could hear the wind whistling in their feathers. Twice blessed and grinning from ear to ear, we boarded the bus and everyone promptly went to sleep on our long journey back to Arequipa.

The next day, after flying to Lima, everyone said fond farewells, marveling at the trip we had just completed. Lena and I embarked on a quick three-day trip to the jungle for a visit with Herlinda and Enrique. The jungle heat was so intense after the cold of the Andes that we could barely move, so we underwent a short diet and quietly lay in hammocks, integrating all that had happened.

On this trip to the Andes we ate, talked, danced, drank, shared, did ceremony, saw new sights, and enjoyed meeting the local people. We celebrated, shopped, prayed, sang, and supported one another in countless little ways. As our guide Puma said over and over again, it's not the way you arrive that matters so much, it's the way you leave that really matters. We left truly happy.

POSTSCRIPT

When real power is truly present, certain signs are unmistakable. One is that weather phenomena are clearly synchronistic with the events taking place. In this case it was the meteor sighting and the great column of wind and dust in the temple just as we began ceremony. You could dismiss these things as mere coincidences but after a while you just cannot dismiss all of them, especially when they are extremely rare events. Another sign that power is at hand is the tendency for everyone present to become telepathic with one another and anticipate and naturally know what to do next. This is hard to explain but is illustrated by the connectedness of the villagers to the moods and intentions of our group when we visited the feminine peak. Nothing was actually announced ahead of time, but somehow everyone knew what was going to happen and how to respond.

EXERCISE

Pay close attention to every little weather phenomenon for the next couple of days. For example, notice what you were thinking just before a sudden breeze came along. What were you saying just as you heard a roll of thunder in the distance, when it started to rain heavily, or when a cloud passed over the sun? See if you can notice a relationship between the natural environment and what you are thinking and feeling.

10

AN ENCOUNTER
WITH POWER THROUGH
A HEALING CRISIS
The Natural Traveling Pharmacy

After returning from three weeks in Peru and resting for only a week at home, I foolishly planned to travel to Russia to carry out an intensive seminar schedule. To make matters more difficult, I was very ill with a virus I came down with on my last day in the jungle. I was to give a two-hour lecture on prosperity, a three-day seminar covering the entire Power Path Personality System (a.k.a. the Michael system), and after a planned day of rest, a two-day seminar called "Being on the Right Track." I did not yet know that a number of other public appearances would be added to my schedule once I got there.

I arrived in Moscow after a thirty-hour journey with a cough that had started in the Amazon and was getting rapidly worse. In a state of complete exhaustion, I knew I had made a terrible mistake in not making sure I was completely healthy before embarking on such a grueling schedule. One of my hosts left me at a hotel near Red Square to rest up. I fought off late calls from various "very special" Russian girls soliciting sex in the lobby, left my phone off the hook, and finally got some sleep.

The next day I had an orientation meeting with my hosts, interviewed various interpreters, and planned the week's events. Late in the afternoon we drove through horrific traffic to a big hall in a bookstore where I was to give the talk on prosperity. Fighting a bad cough on the drive, I tried to go over my talk while in a delirium of jet lag, waves of chills and fever, and trouble breathing the polluted air. I was already losing my voice and wondering if I could make it through the evening. But failure was not an option so, buoyed by the crowd and driven from my head into my heart by my worsening condition, I delivered an outstanding spontaneous talk on prosperity through my interpreter, all the while sucking on cough drops to avoid croaking or screeching my words.

Afterward, I was mobbed with beaming Muscovites wanting me to sign their tattered Russian-edition copies of *Transforming Your Dragons*. To my great surprise the book had sold sixty thousand copies and was being reprinted. I managed to accommodate them amid an incessant flash of cameras, a most strange experience of celebrity when all I wanted was to lie down and sleep. Then there was dinner, conversation, and finally the bliss of bed.

The next day I began the three-day seminar in an ice-cold, drafty hall with seventy people in attendance: therapists, journalists, and other people of importance. I felt cold all day. By late afternoon my voice was failing badly and the mild October weather had become blustery and chilly, threatening to snow. I was woefully unprepared: I needed a long overcoat, a knit hat, and gloves. My kind hosts, seeing my distress, loaned me wool sweaters to keep me warm. I did not want to alarm them by letting on how ill I felt, but I told them I was under the weather with gastrointestinal discomfort, probably due to the abrupt change in climate and the different bacteria in the water.

That night after the seminar in the cold air, I knew my health was crashing. I could feel myself sliding into flu-like symptoms, and when I reached my hotel room I had uncontrollable diarrhea and such waves of illness that I could barely get undressed in the frigid room and flop into a stupor under the covers.

Now I was in sheer panic. I could see no way I could continue the seminar series. I had come all the way to Moscow and was facing a disaster. In my entire career as an international speaker, I had never been in this dilemma before. I was on the verge of calling the front desk and trying to get them to send a doctor to my room to help me immediately. My mind was out of control as I lay there thinking of all the possibilities of what could be wrong with me. Perhaps some terrible jungle disease was blasting forward in full viral or bacterial form. Maybe I was coming down with typhoid, meningitis, dengue fever, or yellow fever. Maybe I had some unnamable disease that doctors in Moscow had no idea how to treat. Might I even die in Moscow because no one would know how to treat me? I pictured Lena flying in just in time to see me expire in some cold hospital with hammers and sickles on the wall.

I had a thermometer with me and discovered that, although I was sweating, I was a full two degrees lower than normal. What could this mean? Thyroid disease? I had a dry cough, backaches, diarrhea, a headache, and waves of weird, bad feelings driving through me, making me feel terribly anxious. Every time I closed my eyes, all I could see was green jungle vines and plants all around me, and I felt the spirit of some alien viral intruder in my body.

I had reached a crisis point, absolute bottom, and had to face reality: I could not tough it out and carry on my ambitious schedule.

I took stock and assessed my situation. Maybe in the morning I would have to tell my hosts how sick I was and cancel. They would take a terrible financial loss; I would offer to compensate them as best I could. Not only would I not earn anything from my trip, but it would cost me a lot of money.

Step one in managing my crisis was that I stopped resisting this idea but instead accepted it and found that I could live with it. Step two consisted of making an inventory of my tools for healing. As I considered my travel pharmacy, I realized I was actually in the same position as most people in the world who had to rely on their wits to get better.

I made a mental inventory:

1. I had a bottle of cough medicine that warned against taking it if blood pressure was low. I deduced from my low body temperature that I had low blood pressure, so the cough medicine was out.

2. I had some cough drops and they were helpful.

3. I had a thermometer to take my temperature.

4. I had some black walnut drops to help get rid of parasites.

5. I had some maca (like ginseng) from Peru.

6. I had a cassette tape of some icaros sung by two different shamans for my protection and healing.

7. I had some Agua Florida in a little bottle containing some icaros given to me by a shaman in Peru.

8. I had some *mapacho*, cigarettes that had been prayed and sung over by the same shaman in Peru.

9. I had a hawk feather I was using as a bookmark.

Then I remembered my most important healing tools:

1. I had my two hands for healing myself.

2. I had the ability to focus my mind toward certain specific subjects.

3. I had the power of my intent and my choice to have a positive attitude. Now I was on a roll. I realized I had some more extraordinary ingredients in my pharmacy.

4. I had my allies, my invisible helpers including Guadalupe, the Huichol teacher I had apprenticed with for ten years and who had passed on.

5. I had knowledge of *chi gong*, an ancient Taoist shamanic practice of accumulating power and energy, and the ability to focus and send my breath where I needed it.

6. Finally, the most powerful ingredient of all was that I had my ability to go within and talk to Spirit.

I had no aspirin, painkillers, or Western medicine of any consequence, yet I realized that I had quite a powerful traveling pharmacy. Immediately I felt stronger and a little better about my predicament, so I went to work. I decided that the first action should be going within and talking to Spirit, or my own essence (the two being basically the same). I opened the dialogue, and to my great satisfaction I made immediate contact. Here is the gist of the conversation that took place.

¤

Me: Well, Spirit, I am in a nasty situation. First of all, I want to thank you for the gift of my life, for creating me and giving me this opportunity to come to Russia. Thank you also for helping me in my time of need. I came all the way over here to keep my agreements and do my life-task work. I have work to do, so I will try my best to fulfill my duty if I possibly can. If not, I will accept my situation and not resist. What do I need to know at this time?

Spirit (or essence): José, indeed you are quite ill. Yet this is not the allotted time for you to die. There is no need to be quite so dramatic. We can help stabilize you and help you get through your obligations here. It will not be easy but it can be done. First, you absolutely must agree to one thing.

Me: Okay, anything. I'm desperate.

Spirit: We can help you, but when you get home you must agree to rest and take time to heal yourself. You must make it your number-one priority. Do not launch headlong into another frenzy of work. You have pushed yourself too hard and too far and you are paying the price.

Me: Okay, agreed. I get it. What else?

Spirit: Right now you must get control over your anxiety and your thoughts. They are not at all helpful, but you can use your mind to your advantage. No matter what, you must not concentrate on your worries. Be in the moment at all costs.

Me: Okay, got it. Sounds hard but I will do it.

Spirit: You are physically sick, but this illness has its roots in the hard work you did in Peru on your lack of unconditional love for yourself. Now you must practice what you learned there. Love yourself no matter what, even if you have to cancel everything.

Me: Tall order, but I get it.

Spirit: Take a very hot bath and then get under the covers and sweat.

Me: Done!

¤

So I began. First I took out my jungle pharmacy and, with affection, doused myself with some aromatic Agua Florida. Then, in a ceremonial manner, I smoked myself with some special tobacco, calling upon my shaman healers in Peru to help me. I called upon Guadalupe and other allies and thanked them for all their help. Then I asked them to help me through the use of my limited but potent tool kit. Using my hawk feather as Guadalupe had taught me, I thoroughly cleansed my body of unwanted or alien energies, concentrating on my chest and throat, where the malady seemed at its worst. Then, using my hands, I gave myself an intense foot and hand massage, concentrating on those points that hurt a lot.

Next, I performed several chi gong exercises that are good for people who are bedridden and ill, including the inner smile, where you create a smile on your face and smile inside at whatever you focus on. This is a powerful technique for strengthening the immune system and shifting stuck patterns.

I found chi gong challenging at first because I was feeling so poorly, but I forced myself to do it and after a time it came more easily. I found something easy to smile at: the mental image of my dog, Russ, sleeping with his head on the cats or looking at me with his big funny ears hanging down. Then I smiled at various parts of my body and at my situation, even laughed out loud at the craziness of it all, despite the fact that I didn't feel very amused.

Then I told my body that I was very sorry I had mistreated it, taken it for granted, and pushed it so hard, and I promised to take better care of it. I told it I loved it and thanked it for all its hard work supporting me over the course of my life. Since I was so sick, my heart was open and this was easy for me to do.

I filled the tub with the hottest water I could stand, got in, and soaked deeply. Climbing out steaming, I dried quickly, staggered over to the bed, and snuggled under the quilts, sweating heavily and soaking the sheets through. As I lay there I worked intensively on my mental state: my focus, intent, and attitude. I disciplined myself to avoid worry and concentrated on getting well. Over and over again I repeated to myself and to what the shamans call the field of intent and physicists call the quantum field, "I am well. I am well. I am healed. I am strong. I am powerful. Spirit, I am in you and you are in me" and on like this creatively.

As I repeated this mantra, I reached an unusually clear mental state. I saw that whatever illness I had was a mental construct: things are thoughts and thoughts are things. Since the body is composed of subatomic particles that wink on and off millions of times a second, appearing only briefly in the present moment, and since what I call "myself" is mostly empty space, the illness must likewise be made up of mostly empty space. I saw that the illness was being created moment by moment and had no real permanence or fixed reality—it was ephemeral in nature. I could also see that I might starve it by withdrawing any mental energy I was giving it. At that moment I remembered the tape with icaros from the jungle. I pulled out my tape recorder and listened to the icaros over and over, singing along with them with all my focus and strength. The Shipibo icaros are designed to work at the subatomic level, clearing away maladies and foreign energies and inserting healing frequencies. With an enormous sense of relief, I could feel them working: clearing, cleaning, purifying, raising the vibratory level of key points in my body. I could sense that the illness the icaros were clearing out was indeed a tendency to be deeply critical of myself, a legacy of early childhood held over and still operating in the now point. I patted my body all over and felt great compassion for it, realizing that it was my responsibility to heal myself and I could do that with the tools I had with me. I was truly amazed at what I was learning at the deepest experiential level. Finally, I drifted off to sleep.

In the morning I awoke very weak, very delicate, and still sick, but "better." I slowly got dressed, and by the time my host came to pick me up for the seminar, I believed I could actually carry off teaching until at least noon. I was honest with her and told her that I had been very ill but assured her I would do my best. I could see the look of genuine fear on her face, so I did what I could to calm her down. She was kind enough to inform a doctor friend, who brought me some homeopathic drops that proved to be quite helpful in the coming days.

I arrived at the hall fortified with warm clothes and began the seminar. Soon I got into the swing of lecturing, answering questions, and interviewing audience members about their "overleaves," or personality traits. Their genuine openness and willingness to reveal themselves in such a public forum was so inspiring to me that I forgot all about being sick. At the end of the day I remembered my agreement with Spirit and declined all the Saturday night invitations to go out, instead returning to my hotel room for more work on myself using my tools and to get a good night's rest.

I was definitely not well, but I was incredibly relieved and grateful to be able to carry on with the seminars and my work. The chill I got and my coughing had pulled a rib out and twisted a vertebra in my neck, causing me a lot of pain. I figured I was being sorely tested and reminded myself not to get too complacent. Nevertheless, I genuinely began to enjoy the whole experience of being in Moscow teaching, lecturing, and meeting so many interesting people.

I completed the third day and had a day off before the next seminar began. I was well enough to go to Red Square and see a little of the city. The next seminar took place in a different hotel. We had a powerful two-day experience that included many chi gong exercises—rather difficult for me with my pulled rib but nevertheless manageable.

I was finally done and had met all my obligations—or so I thought. My hosts had enthusiastically arranged for a lecture at Moscow State University, the most prestigious university in Russia. I was to deliver a three-hour talk to some seventy faculty members of all disciplines on the subject of communication. Stunned, I realized I had left my notes on this subject back in Santa Fe, not thinking I would need them. I quickly drew up what materials I did have and wrote down as much as I could remember from my notes, and then went out to give a lecture to a highly educated and possibly highly critical audience. Nevertheless, a strange calm settled over me as I walked into a state-of-the-art theater-style classroom with big-screen TVs hanging from the ceiling.

After what I presumed was a fancy introduction given with a flourish by my host Anatoli, a doctor of psychology, I began my talk with the help of an interpreter. I told the audience that I preferred not to use jargon, and my talk would not be heavy on research and scientific language. I preferred to use simple practical language to make straightforward points about a subject that could be very beneficial to them. I mentioned that I had discovered in my own life that the most useful information is often the simplest. I then proceeded with my lecture, hoping they would agree with my observations. From the many smiling faces and nods, I deduced that things were going well. Then it was break time and Anatoli drew me aside and nervously suggested that I give them more complex material because he was worried that it might be too simple.

After all, this was his class and he wanted to make sure they would be satisfied and challenged. Again, I felt strangely calm and understood completely that there was no problem but that I would have to somehow satisfy this concern.

I told the class that they might think my concepts were very simple but that it was part of a much bigger system of understanding people, and I was sharing only a very small but important part of it. I launched into value systems and different ways of perceiving the world. I mentioned seven attitudes, modes, needs, and fear patterns that could easily block meaningful attempts to communicate. By this time the class participants were writing furiously in their notebooks, and hands were shooting up everywhere. I could see that they were beginning to glimpse a much larger way of perceiving people and how vast the topic of communication really was. Then I finished the lecture after answering many questions and giving them practical advice about how to teach more effectively. To my great relief, they were very grateful and happy and I felt a deep satisfaction surge over me. I had a clear sense that I was doing my life-task work and that I had just fulfilled a major set of agreements with a group of people in a far-off land. *Aaahhhh.* Seventy more agreements completed. How many yet to go?

POSTSCRIPT
The Essence of the Natural Traveling Pharmacy

Not everyone is going to just happen to have a tape of icaros from the Amazon with them, nor is everyone going to carry a hawk feather, Agua Florida, maca, mapacho, or black walnut drops or have knowledge of chi gong. These just happen to be in my pharmacy but you may have different tools in yours. So let's concentrate on the most important ingredients of the pharmacy that almost everyone has at all times:

1. Two hands for healing

2. The choice to focus your mind toward specific subjects

3. The focus of your breath

4. The power of intent using a positive attitude

5. Various allies, invisible helpers, if you believe they exist for you

6. The ability to go within and talk to Spirit, if you believe this exists for you

If you have no problem with numbers 5 and 6, you have six powerful tools at your disposal. If you do have trouble with 5 and 6, you have at least four tools. If you are too much of a skeptic, you may be in real trouble.

Each day that passes reveals to me more clearly that the most powerful device in the universe is the mind: the ability to think, feel, and intend. This is what programs the quantum field, or field of intent, to magnetize itself into specific forms or manifestations that we then experience as reality moment by moment. This is what allows us to create and re-create our experience at will.

It has been said that we human beings are made in the image and likeness of our creator. I believe this has nothing to do with our appearance but rather refers to our minds, which are able to create at will using the power of intention. We can intend to use our hands for clearing, opening, organizing, unblocking, and circulating energy. With our hands we can nurture, perform direct healing, and make powerful gestures that shape a new reality, like a wizard waving a wand.

Even if we are missing our hands, we can still imagine them with intent. With our focus and intent we can choose to re-create our experience, and with a shift of attitude we have the power of the universe at our disposal. A relationship with allies extends this power infinitely, and ultimately the ability to speak directly to Spirit grants us access to wisdom—important information that we may need in the moment to guide us to make better choices.

Through an uncomfortable illness in a challenging time, I was granted a rare and great opportunity to learn a great deal about my core resources and how to apply them effectively. Once again I was reminded that the price of becoming more powerful is leaving my comfort zone. I hope that my sharing this experience with you will make your own traveling pharmacy more accessible to you when you need it.

EXERCISE

At random times, check in and see if you can identify the forms of medicine at your disposal in the natural pharmacy of nature: sunshine, shade, moisture, heat, the presence of an animal, a person, and so on. Even if you are not outside, check out what is in the pharmacy of your life, including your own medicinal thoughts, attitudes, insights, and feelings. Realize that you are surrounded by medicines everywhere, all the time.

PART III

ACTION
Chief-Warrior

The chief is the leader within, the one who takes responsibility for being clear about what direction to take. Having clarity and being calm in the face of a crisis are hallmarks of the chief. In ancient times, all emperors of China were trained shamans. This was true in many other traditions as well. They were powerful leaders who knew how to use their intuition and had a deep connection with the natural world.

The warrior aspect of the shaman is disciplined, focused, organized, and action-oriented. In the chaos of battle the warrior keeps what is important in focus and, despite setbacks, makes relentless progress until the mission is accomplished. For the shaman, the battle is within, not with external enemies.

Jesus spent forty days and forty nights in the desert battling his own demons in order to get clear about what lay ahead for him. Siddhartha Gautama sat under the Bodhi tree fighting off his egoic demons until he emerged weeks later as the enlightened Buddha. Shamans battle not only their own demons but the demons that possess the personalities of their patients. Great healers are able to cast out demons.

While some of the stories in part III have ceremonies taking place within them, I chose to put them under the chief-warrior axis because of the challenges that had to be faced. These stories all have to do with taking charge, taking responsibility, or dealing with demons of various sorts, for better or worse. Fighting a battle is not always pretty but the important thing is to win it.

11

AN ENCOUNTER
WITH POWER

Completing a Huichol
Apprenticeship with Sacred Peyote

W hen our Huichol teacher and *maracame* (shaman) Guadalupe passed away, Lena and I had not yet finished the final ceremony that would complete our ten years of study with him that we began in the late 1980s. As he lay dying, we made the two-day drive from Santa Fe to high in the Sierras of central Mexico to visit him one last time. He lay in his bed in a small, crowded cinder-block hut where his family lived with their few belongings. Guadalupe was experiencing a great deal of pain from bone cancer, relieved from time to time by morphine injections administered by his son.

Incredibly, he managed to laugh and show his great sense of humor despite his illness. After visiting with him for a time, we gently asked him what we should do to complete our apprenticeship after he was gone. He said that we should make one last journey to the Huichol peyote fields in the harsh desert of Wirikuta, on the anniversary of the day we had observed ceremonies each year. There we should go to the usual place in the desert, the place with the tall Joshua trees standing like sentinels, and follow all the protocols for the all-night ceremony just as he had shown us.

With a great effort he addressed us. "I will join you there. Don't worry. You will finish. You are ready. You must teach. You must show people the way."

"But what if you don't get better and you can't come after all?" I asked, my voice faltering.

"Don't worry," he repeated. "I will be there," adding, "even if I die."

We both nodded, somewhat mollified. "Okay," we said.

He seems to know what he is talking about. Who are we to question? I thought. I certainly knew that by now.

Our stay with him was poignant. He was in great pain but we wanted to be near him, knowing we would never be with him again in his physical form. His family doted over him lovingly and took pains to see that we were taken care of too. Guadalupe supervised them in making a bed for us on the floor. That night a terrific rainstorm swept the mountains, and we were grateful for the shelter inside.

During our stay, we were invited to a fertility corn festival about an hour's walk through the forest to another Huichol village. We hiked with his son Rafael to the village through rugged but beautiful terrain of pine forests. Long, open vistas of the Sierras stretched out ahead of us. As we neared the village, Rafael told us to stop and wait while he entered to get final permission for us to join the ceremony. We could hear drums and singing coming from the village below. While we were waiting, a dark Huichol man with an old torn shirt came down the trail from another direction leading a heavily laden donkey piled with wood. He hailed us, and upon reaching us stopped, looked at us earnestly, and said in Spanish, "And what has God told you today?" A bit shocked, having never before been addressed this way, I mumbled something about it being a good day.

He listened and then said God told him that this is a time of great change for human beings, that there would be flooding in many parts of the world, and that many people would die because people are not living right anymore. Not everyone would die, however. Those living in the mountains would be safe. He said we must return to living in proper harmony with the earth. He continued in this fashion until Rafael returned from the village announcing that we had received approval to enter. Rafael and the man greeted each other warmly and exchanged pleasantries. We bade the man farewell, and as we trudged toward the village I asked Rafael who the man was. He told us that the man with the donkey was his uncle and was known as a powerful seer and prophet among his people. He said it was most fortunate that we had a chance to meet him. I thought about the chances of bumping into him in this vast, rugged country with no roads, only foot trails, and realized that it was not an accident. Our paths were destined to cross.

We entered the village to an amazing sight. A number of older maracames were performing healings on small children in the afternoon sun. Accompanying their activities were drummers beating out a cadence on several large wooden drums whose skins were drawn taut by a small fire built beneath each one. The maracames, elder women and men, were using their powerful *movieris* (feather wands) to extract illness and other maladies from the children. Meanwhile, food was being prepared in large clay urns placed over other fires. Smoke, hot sun, drumming, and singing filled the air as dozens of Huichol dressed in brightly colored clothing sat or stood watching the healings or preparing food. Looking around, I saw no white people and only a couple of people who looked Mexican but not Indian.

The village stood perched on the side of a rugged escarpment, and a deep chasm dropped away below. The stupendous view formed a backdrop for the proceedings. We watched for hours as the maracames tirelessly performed their services, taking great care with the children and infants who at times wailed as they were being blessed. Rafael told us that this healing and blessing of children always took place at the fertility festival this time of year. They saw the children as intimately associated with the well-being of the village and the overall harvest. I had a profound sense of how fortunate we were to witness such a powerful event while our teacher and friend lay dying in the neighboring village.

As night fell, the air chilled and the healings ended. The area was cleared for dances but not before the feast was served. We were ushered into a large thatch-roofed hut and sat on benches along the walls. Bowls were handed out and the Huichol came around bearing large pots from which a thick, delicious venison soup was served into each waiting bowl. We were provided as many small corn tortillas as we could consume. Many of the Huichol looked at us curiously but in a friendly sort of way. They treated us with great hospitality.

After we ate, a drunk young Huichol man staggered into the hut and stood swaying before us, a look of hatred in his reddened eyes. In a loud, slurred voice he aggressively demanded to know what we were doing there. At first we tried to ignore him, but it became apparent that he was not leaving until we answered his question. I told him in Spanish that we were guests of Rafael and that we had obtained permission to participate. This deterred him not at all, and he proceeded to loudly deride and insult us as gringos and foreigners who he said had no right to be there. He was making such a racket that all conversations stopped and all eyes turned toward this unpleasant drama.

The lovely gathering had now become a tense confrontation. While I experienced some fear, I also tried to remember what I had learned from Guadalupe about dealing with such situations. I relaxed as much as I could and visualized sending the man a bouquet of flowers as a gesture of peace. Of course, on an external level this produced no results at all, as he continued to rail against us and gesture threateningly toward Lena and me. At one point I got up to leave the room because I could see no other recourse, but at this point an elder Huichol intervened on our behalf and gestured that I should sit back down. He told the man that this was no way to treat guests and that he should leave us be. A great discussion ensued as other Huichol joined in and exhorted him to stand down. I began to understand how these indigenous people dealt with conflict in their community. There were no attempts to forcibly remove the drunken man or treat him with disrespect, only to persuade him to behave properly. After what seemed like a long time, he staggered away and we were left in peace. The party resumed as if nothing had happened. We eventually went outside to watch the dancing, but I kept my eyes open for any more trouble from the drunken man.

Eventually we found Rafael and told him what had happened. He explained that alcohol was making its way into remote villages and was a problem for the people. He also told us that the young Indian was a troublemaker and a known murderer. Aghast, I asked him how the people handled criminals in their midst. He replied that the Mexican laws and police had no impact in these out-of-the-way areas and that the people simply had to resolve these things for themselves.

The Huichol have a security force but there is no official Mexican government court system, so they try to settle problems with dialogue. They have their own informal court system manned by elders and elected representatives who agree to do it without compensation. Sometimes it means that the atypical murderer continues to live among them.

After hearing him speak, I realized what danger we had been in. I also understood tearfully that even though Guadalupe was dying, he was watching over us and shamanically protecting us in that village. I told Lena how incredibly grateful I felt and she agreed. Late that night after a full and heartfelt day, we returned by moonlight over the rugged terrain to our village where we slept briefly until a cacophony of roosters, goats, sheep, and braying donkeys woke us up well before dawn.

◻

Our journey with Guadalupe first began in 1989 when, through his brother Mariano, an expert yarn painter, we met him in Berkeley. He was working in the back of a small rock shop doing healings. He spoke no English but could get by in Spanish, his second language, and we were able to communicate with him marginally. We both got *limpias* (cleansings) from him and enjoyed our visit with him immensely. It was obvious from the start that he had other ways of communicating and words in any language were secondary.

A few days later, Mariano let us know that Guadalupe was open to working with a few students. He would work with couples, and were we interested? We both jumped at the chance and gave our unqualified yes, having no idea what we would be in for. Soon we learned how arduous the path of apprenticeship was. Three couples committed to a path of five years. One was Ecuadorian and the other was gringo like us. Sometimes Guadalupe would come up from his home in Mexico by bus, and sometimes we would make the long drive down to his home territory to do ceremony with him deep in Mexico. Guadalupe asserted that we all had to be present to carry out any ceremony, and because we all had young children, sometimes we could not make the journey at the time suggested. In the end, the five-year apprenticeship took ten years, and when not all the couples could continue, he relented and agreed to work with just Lena and me because of our strong interest and commitment to the path. We were also the only ones who persistently paid his expenses.

Because Guadalupe was a high maracame, it was not politically correct for him to have North Americans as apprentices, but he was very open-minded and did not consider nationality important. He did, however, need to swear us to secrecy: we were not to mention our apprenticeship with him to anyone—no exceptions. He would mention to no one his work with us. In order to avoid the other Huichol groups, we had to go to the desert to do ceremony at the least clement time of year when no one else was there. Needless to say, we froze our asses off in the November winds that swept across the peyote fields of Mexico. By dawn our bodies would be covered with hoarfrost as we shivered with cold, faces and hands blackened by the guttering fire, praying for the sunrise that took forever to come. On the other hand, the first rays of the sun onto the desert could only be described as glorious and earth-shattering after we had prayed and sung all night with Grandfather Hikuri (peyote). Sometimes the dawn was cloudy and we continued to freeze, shaking off chunks of ice from our ponchos and hats. Nevertheless, I would not trade those frozen desert dawns for the world, so powerful and transforming were they.

Guadalupe inspired us and became a role model for us, as he never wore socks with his sandals during these freezing ceremonies. At times we took pity on him and lent him a down jacket since he had nothing but his cotton shirt and pants to ward off the cold.

Upon completing the dawn ritual of blessing with seawater, we would head up to the mountains to make offerings and complete other prayers. As I found out, the shamanic path requires you to be in good physical condition, and if you are not in shape, it tests you intensely. Because one of the couples was very out of shape, they could not make such journeys and eventually dropped out. Once, they took the bus all the way down into Mexico within miles of our meeting place but lost their passports, forcing them to cancel at the last minute. Such events tend to weed out who finishes and who does not.

◻

A couple of weeks after our visit with Guadalupe on his death-bed, he passed away. It was late May 1999. We received the news quietly and accepted it, but inwardly I was devastated. Guadalupe had become so important to me as a teacher that I felt completely at a loss about what to do. I was taken aback by how hard I was taking the loss. I had doubts about my abilities, about my readiness, about how I would learn with him gone. I felt like I didn't know anything at all. I found myself spontaneously crying at various times and yet, because we had kept our apprenticeship a secret for so long, it was difficult to share this loss with many people. For the most part, Lena and I shouldered it alone. Even today as I write this, my eyes are filled with tears and I feel an overwhelming sense of gratitude, loss, and amazement all at once.

As the year went by, I felt more and more ambivalent about our final ceremony in Wirikuta. I couldn't wait to go back to the place where we had experienced such power with Guadalupe, but at the same time I dreaded going there, knowing we would be in the desert alone this time, without any members of our group and without his wonderful presence. Finally the day came for Lena and me to pack the car and once again make the thirteen-hundred-mile trip to the Sonoran Desert deep in Mexico. The drive was actually healing in that we had become familiar with so many landmarks, truck stops, motels, and cafés along the way. Each leg of the trip held familiar places and memories.

We arrived in Catorce in the evening, a dusty railroad station town with nothing but a small Pemex gas station, barren streets, and the occasional mongrel dog lurking about. From there, Wadley was a hop, skip, and a jump, another dismal railroad town but nevertheless the entryway to Wirikuta, sacred ceremonial lands to all Huichol. (The town bears the unlikely name of Wadley after an American miner who established it as an outpost.) We drove to the café across from the primitive cinder block motel and ordered up some tortillas and rice. The family recognized us from many prior visits, and soon we left our car in their fenced compound. The old patron Carlos joked and laughed with us just like old times, and we arranged for him to take us out the next day in his pickup truck to the usual place where he would drop us off.

By mid-afternoon the next day we were bumping down the dirt road toward the ceremonial site in Carlos's ancient multi-colored pickup truck, clouds of dust and burning oil enveloping the miraculous wreckage. The destination in the creosote bush and Joshua tree desert landscape was a good seven miles from the village. The deep ruts were filled with a powdered dust that billowed up from the tires in choking clouds that penetrated the cab of the truck, covering backpacks, clothes, and water bottles in beige grit. The rolled-up windows had long since lost their handles, making it stifling in the bright ninety-degree heat of a winter day. We sat four across the bench seat—Carlos, his nephew, Lena, and me. Still, we were happy to be here at last, going to the ceremony site for the last time to complete our apprenticeship. As we wound through a couple of outlying ranches, the truck suddenly ground to a halt.

"We have to stop here," the portly Carlos stated suddenly. "The road ahead is blocked. They are doing construction with a bulldozer and we can't go further. You can walk from here. It's not far." Looking out ahead, I could see nothing blocking the road, and it seemed strange that he was dropping us off a good mile before the usual drop-off place. But I figured he had a reason. After arranging to be picked up in the morning, we bid our farewells and hefted our packs for the walk in.

Laden with supplies we had not expected to have to carry in our decrepit old packs, we headed down the road and eventually turned off into the scrubby desert to reach the ceremonial site, navigating through spiny cactus whose seedpods seemed to leap out and grab boots and pierce shirts and pants. We followed burro and goat trails that wound through the cactus and crisscrossed everywhere. Eventually we came to the Joshua tree forest and found the exact tree overlooking the little area we had cleared in years past. From this vantage point we could see the full desert for a good thirty miles along with the rugged range of mountains to our east. There in plain sight rose Cerro Quemado with its double peaks in the shape of deer antlers, most sacred of mountains and the destination of thousands of Huichol every year. In two days' time we would climb to its top as we did each year to complete our pilgrimage. The view was nothing short of spectacular.

The reddish late-afternoon light slanted across the landscape, making everything appear ablaze, a phenomenon we liked to call "golden time." We set up our altar and arranged our ceremonial things and our sleeping bags and ponchos for the long night ahead. In November the night air turns very cold, and with nothing to stop it the wind can howl for hours on end. We braced ourselves for what we had experienced in years past: a harsh, unforgiving night in the desert. With very little burnable wood, we had to scrounge for cactus skeletons and enough small twigs to keep a little fire going all night long. This was very hard work, and before we were finished

I had to pull quite a few thorns and cactus spines out of my hands and legs.

Then we set out to look for the ceremonial peyote cactus buttons that were an important ingredient for the ceremony. We had to find seven plants apiece. Looking for Grandfather Peyote is like a treasure hunt. According to the Huichol, the Great Spirit came to this land long ago in the form of Kauyumari, the great blue deer and original shaman who taught the Huichol everything they knew. It descended from the sky and jumped across the landscape. Everywhere its feet touched, there grew the sacred peyote, the plant form of the sun given to the Huichol so they could become wise and discover the universe. According to Guadalupe, not every peyote plant would do for ceremonial purposes. We had to look for particular peyote growing in a certain configuration.

The peyote can hide from you if it does not want to be seen. Guadalupe had told us that you have to hunt for it with an open heart and only then would it reveal itself. This was like hunting for deer but in plant form. We carried our sacred movieris like the arrows with which to hunt. I looked and looked but for a long time could find nothing. I began to worry because the sun had gone down and soon it would be dark. I realized that my heart was not open because of my irritation with the unplanned hike to get there and my worry over doing everything right without Guadalupe. I had to stop and clear these things out of my mind before I could go on with the hunt. I asked my allies for help and they reminded me to sing. I whistled and softly sang to the peyote, asking it to come and thanking it. Immediately I found them. Lena was having no trouble at all. Our hunt was successful.

After preparing the cactus in the special way that Guadalupe had shown us and placing it upon the altar, we prepared other ceremonial items that required tying small items to prayer sticks, a very difficult task with wind blowing dust in our eyes while our fingers froze in the desert chill. We started the fire and were fortunate that the wind calmed down and the night was not as frightfully cold as it had been. The moon rose gloriously over the desert, and in the far distance we could see the lights of the trains traveling very slowly across the plain below, occasionally sounding their mournful horns in the blue-black night. Coyotes yelped and cried in the distance and a light breeze ruffled the desert plants. The desert was coming alive.

The ceremony called for us to consume peyote five times throughout the night. Each time is always more difficult than the last. Guadalupe had exhorted us to eat as many buttons as possible to successfully meet with the grandfather. He could seemingly eat a limitless amount, but for us it was more difficult. The fresh peyote is very alkaline, and it is difficult to keep it down and not purge violently and often. Keeping a little bit in the cheek at all times and praying as each piece is consumed helps greatly.

Guadalupe called the peyote *hikuri* and said that each one of the light-blue cactuses was a representative of the sun. They sat in the desert absorbing the sunlight for years, and when we consumed them we were literally eating sunlight. In addition to the sun, each peyote represented Kauyumari. The hikuri is also linked with fertility and corn that feeds the people; it represents the corn maiden, whose hair is the same as the silk on a husk of corn. He told us eating the hikuri was participating in all these things that are linked in the minds of the Huichol. He always commented on how beautiful these ideas were.

Sometime around midnight my attention was drawn to a spot on the other side of the small fire in front of us. Suddenly I heard my name spoken as clear as can be. I looked to see if Lena had spoken to me but she clearly had not; she had covered her head with a blanket to keep warm and was deep in visions.

Then I heard it again and I looked back to the spot across the fire. Guadalupe sat there grinning broadly. I could hardly believe my eyes. It was one of the strangest things I have ever experienced because he was there but I could see the desert and landscape right through him. It was as if I was seeing him in my mind but he was also there at that spot. He beckoned me, and I got up and went over to him. He said very clearly, "I told you I would come." I was so overwhelmed that I burst into tears. I told him how happy I was to see him. He just smiled and told me he had a great many important things to tell me.

For the next four hours or so, we had a powerful and amazing conversation about many topics. At first he was very tough on me like he could be at times and told me exactly what work I needed to do on myself to become more powerful. He targeted ways I had been lazy and fearful and told me this would never do. He told me I fantasized and worried too much and this demonstrated my lack of faith, something I could ill afford if I wanted to grow. I had work to do on this and he expected me to do it.

I felt sobered but not defensive at all. I was so happy he was there that I listened attentively and in total agreement. After what seemed like a long time, he told me that I was a great human being and that I was much loved by Spirit. He told me I had a great deal to contribute and that I would receive much help from both him and others to get this work done. I was in tears during most of this conversation. Just before dawn he said I should take a little rest and that he would not go away. In fact, he said that for as long as I wanted, he would always be with me as a helper.

I was so energized and amazed that when I went back to the fire and lay down, I could not rest much at all. Finally, Lena uncovered herself and I excitedly told her what had transpired. To my amazement she said she had been talking to Guadalupe too but he appeared to her in a different way, not so externally. I realized that he had been working with both of us at the same time, and of course this would be no problem for him since he was no longer confined to his physical body.

Dawn burst with a rare beauty, and we completed the final obligations of our ceremony. Lena pulled an orange and a couple of bananas out of her pack and we broke our fast. We also took some salt to end our ten-day salt fast. We packed up and, with a confusion of feelings, threaded our way back to the pickup spot. I felt so happy to see Guadalupe, to have our amazing conversation, and to finally complete our ten-year apprenticeship. I was also sad because I didn't know if we would ever come back to this place again and because this challenge that had been so difficult and rewarding was now over.

We plopped ourselves down by the side of the road, finished our water, and waited for the pickup truck. Hours went by. The truck was never this late. It had always been on time in years past, so something was not right. We decided that perhaps the truck was waiting for us where it had dropped us off. So we hefted our packs and grunted down the road in the blazing sun after a night of no sleep, with our water gone, and with nothing left to eat.

We arrived at the drop-off spot and found no sign of the truck. We waited another hour as it got hotter. Finally, with a sinking feeling, we realized that the truck was not coming and we would have to walk the remaining six miles back to town. I was very concerned because of the weight of our packs, the heat, and our physical condition; both of us were still reeling with the effects of the powerful peyote. We plodded down the road, the dust crisscrossed with sidewinder tracks. Vultures spun around over our heads.

I was beginning to feel very sorry for myself when suddenly in my mind's eye I saw Guadalupe on the road walking just ahead of us. I was quite startled to see him again and asked, "¿Qué passa?"

(What's happening?) He said simply, "Huicholes walk." In that moment I knew exactly what was going on. This was our completion. It was not meant to be easy. Naturally there would be an initiation. I realized then that it was Guadalupe who had interfered with the truck coming. The whole crazy story about the bulldozer blocking the road earlier was his doing too. We would have to walk and that was all there was to it.

Suddenly I stopped feeling sorry for myself, remembering his teachings from the night before. Now the walk was serious business and I had to step up to the plate. I told Lena what I saw and she just laughed. Of course, she could see it too. That walk was one of the most difficult I can remember. We had not one drop of water to drink, the sun was blazing, and we'd had no sleep. But somehow we did it, and Guadalupe walked with us every step of the way. When we finally got into town we headed directly for the café. Carlos's wife, Candelaria, stared at us and asked us if we had walked and we told her we had. She said her husband had an emergency in the next town, so he told his nephew to pick us up instead. The nephew had flaked out.

Candelaria prepared us a nice meal and we drank to our hearts' content. Then we packed up the car and headed back to the United States. We drove straight through, thirteen hundred miles to Santa Fe, all day and all night. I never felt tired at all. I knew something profound had happened and life would never quite be the same again. In a way, it was as if my life had begun anew. I was fifty-two years old, the Mayan number of completion.

Now, many years later, Guadalupe has kept his promise and has continued to work with us and support us whenever we need him. I often see him standing nearby when we are conducting ceremonies and doing healing work. Sometimes he will come close and give us a pointer or word of advice, but he is never intrusive. He told us he would visit us in the form of a hummingbird, and he has done this on numerous occasions.

Some of our students report that he has appeared to them this way and is a principal teacher for them. He has even sent us another Huichol teacher who now conducts our ceremonies with us and has taken over what Guadalupe could not finish teaching us.

Several months ago on a very difficult diet in the jungle, he visited me and gave me a wonderful energetic gift that has proven to be very helpful to me. I am most grateful to him and his amazing tradition.

As it has turned out, I have returned to Wirikuta yearly ever since, and the learning goes on and on. I am most fortunate to be on this grand adventure, as I am sure you are on yours.

POSTSCRIPT

Too many of us are afraid to embrace power. We look around and see the abuse of power all around us and decide that power is a bad thing to be avoided. However, if we avoid acquiring power, we learn nothing about it until we face it, experience it, flounder, and then learn to master it. All the greatest of the world's teachers—including Krishna, Jesus, the Buddha, Yogananda, Lao-Tzu, Quan Yin, Isis, and many others—learned to master power, and the world is a better place as a result of their teachings. On their way to mastery, they all failed many times, just as each of us does. Even Jesus struggled to overcome a hot temper when he was a child.

The abuses of power conducted in all these teachers' names came from followers who failed to master the teachings properly. Instead, they made the teachings into codified religions. Before you can become a master teacher yourself, you must learn to master power. But you will not arrive at mastery by following someone else's rules; rather, it will come from your own experience with power.

What are the lessons of this long shamanic journey? They are too numerous for me to list, and some apply only to Lena and me. Yet there are lessons that are typical of the shamanic path. Here is what I learned about power that I can share here:

- Expect the unexpected.

- Discipline and perseverance on the path pay big dividends.

- The price for power is your own comfort.

- Don't whine and complain. It doesn't help.

- The greatest teachings have no words.

- Listen to your teacher's criticisms and learn.

- Open your heart and shed your tears.

- Sing often and never hesitate to pray. Pray with sincere tears in your eyes.

- Take your medicine and learn.

- Watch your routines and habitual responses and see how they limit you.

- Ask your allies for help.

- Let go of attachment to form and you will gain immeasurably.

- Learn by doing and experiencing.

- Don't expect all your learning to come from
  your teacher.

Guadalupe used to say, "I can teach you nothing. Go out there into the mountains and the desert. There you will learn."

There are many teachers. The greatest of them is Mother Nature.

EXERCISE

Remember a time when you were confronted by danger and you felt you needed help. Who were your allies? Did you have access to them at the time? Were you able to call upon any inner allies? Who would you call upon now if something were to happen? Do you trust these allies?

12

A SECOND PILGRIMAGE TO REGALIA

Encounters with the Dark Shaman

In mid-April of the year following my first trip to diet with ayahuasca, I returned to Regalia on the banks of the Rio Respata, Pierre's special diet outpost in the deep jungle of the upper Amazon in Peru, bringing a group of nine people. After I had returned to the States and shared my experiences with students and friends, to my surprise many wanted to go too. So here we were, back and ready for adventure. Our purpose was again to do a special diet under the guidance of two shamans, Pierre and his assistant, the elderly Don Niko. As before, the diet was to cleanse the body and then develop the foundation to work with various plant allies for healing and support. It was for older souls who had already done sufficient shamanic work such that they could endure the rigors of a diet in a harsh jungle environment, remote from any medical facility or communication network. The group consisted of two server types, three creative artisans, two strong kings, two entertaining sages, and one scholar—a highly exalted group, with more than the usual number of servers to nurture and support. It turned out to be a magical combination.

For each traveler, the journey began the moment they agreed to go to Peru. Many fears and obstacles including illness had to be overcome. I myself was so sick with the flu the day before we left that I thought I couldn't go.

From Lima we flew across the Andes to acclimate for a couple of days at Pierre's beautiful botanical gardens in the jungle town of Pucallpa. There we were treated to wonderful, healthy, home-cooked pre-diet meals of fresh fish, grains, soups, and tropical fruits. In town we shopped for hammocks, tobacco, and other things we would need for the deep jungle experience.

The astrology for the trip indicated there would be many obstacles of a physical nature, mainly caused by earth and water, but the group experience would be supportive, especially if perseverance and discipline were applied. We discussed this as a group in order to be prepared for the challenges to come.

That night a rare cold front blew in from the Andes, and for a day we had heavy, cold rain and strong winds. The humidity of the Amazon made it feel much colder, and we bundled up in jackets and blankets. Early the next day we piled into two four-wheel-drive trucks and headed northwest to our destination: the most idyllic jungle camp any of us had ever seen. Much building and clearing had been done since I had been here the year before. Set by a beautiful waterfall and pond, the camp consisted of small two-person shelters covered by palm fronds surrounding a tiny central plaza. There was an open-sided conical ceremonial hut, a shelter for dining, and a small cookhouse. A remote outhouse completed the camp.

There we spent the next seven days slowing down, lounging in hammocks, taking plant baths, and dieting on river fish, plantains, rice, oatmeal, and beans. We could hike through the jungle on machete-cut trails or float up the stream in a small dugout to watch salad plate–sized butterflies float about. On alternate nights we stayed up for several hours participating in intense ceremonies with plant medicines from the jungle. The seventy-four-year-old Don Niko, accompanied by Pierre, sang icaros, blew tobacco on us, and cleaned up our energy throughout the dark night. They were both able to "see" challenges and themes in our lives that they would explain to us the next day if we asked.

Because everyone in the group was interested in the Michael Teachings, also known as the Personessence System (see my website, thepowerpath.com, for more resources), around mealtimes we would discuss a great many personal experiences and learn more about the Michael Teachings through questions and answers. These informative discussions helped the group members understand one another better and thus facilitated our getting along under intense circumstances. The system had been tested by the rigors of the jungle and proved immeasurably useful yet again.

All in all, our group coped exceedingly well and we forged a strong bond. The challenges came in the form of internal emotional struggles, physical discomfort, insects, heat, and encounters with a dark shaman among us.

On the first evening upon our arrival, after we had settled in, the sun was setting and we hurriedly prepared for our ceremony, to be held on the ground underneath a palm frond roof held up with poles. Suddenly out of the jungle a giant bird-eating black tarantula the size of a dinner plate arrived and began to flit around camp at great speed, exploring and most likely looking for a ready meal. People were screaming and running helter-skelter trying to get away. The spider, obviously scared, held up its forelegs wherever it ran, making it look more menacing than ever. Eventually we lost it in the darkness.

Then it was time to sit on the ground and begin the ceremony. Since the ceremony was conducted in complete darkness and there was no moon, we could see nothing. I couldn't quite get the spider out of my mind, and I know others were quite preoccupied with it as well. Every time I reached for my handkerchief to wipe the sweat off my face and clean up my running nose, I was terrified I would put my hand on a furry back, and of course the fantasy was that the spider would climb up my arm and perhaps jump on my face and bite me something fierce, a fate that never actually happened.

When things like this occur at the beginning of or during a ceremony, it is never an accident. The spider helped us all by bringing up some of our instinctive fears, which the medicine would deal with. In the morning all of us agreed, some rather grimly, that the spider had been a major player in the ceremony. It had done its job well.

One day, after we had participated in several ceremonies, Pierre announced that we were going to hike through the jungle to check out some alternative places where we could hold that evening's ceremony. We spent the better part of the afternoon tramping through spectacular scented jungle, wading through warm streams, and slipping and sliding on slick muddy animal trails. I felt somewhat nervous wading through the streams because Pierre had told us that caiman (alligator-like reptiles) lived in these waters, as well as poisonous snakes and dreaded piranha. He told us not to worry about the piranha because it was the wrong time of year for them to attack and they were more scattered. He said it was only during August, the mating season, that they were inclined to unprovoked attacks in aggressive schools. This made me feel only slightly safer.

I remembered seeing a documentary about caiman on the Discovery Channel a few months before and had been surprised to learn how ferocious they were; a little caiman only two feet long could bite your hand off. The fact that, with a headlamp, I had seen the glowing emerald green eyes of a caiman in the water the night before didn't ease my absolutely focused attention on every bubble and ripple. Nevertheless, the enchantment of colorful parrots flying overhead, the magnificently tall hardwood trees, butterflies the size of robins, the powerful lines of leafcutter ants, and the musky scent of the humid jungle made the risk worth taking.

We visited several beautiful secluded sites and eventually settled on a picturesque sandbank along a riffle on a side stream. Looking around and seeing the jungle looming along both banks, I anticipated the night's ayahuasca ceremony with relish. Here we would be that much more intimate with the jungle and its mostly hidden wildlife. As the afternoon was getting on, we headed back to the compound to collect our pads and the few things we needed for the ceremony. Although we were not far from the compound, the route was not easy to traverse, and to get there we had to go up and down some steep ravines with water flowing through them. The slippery, muddy sides required us to manhandle ourselves up with vines and abrasive branches. In one particularly steep ravine, we had to cross by balancing along the slippery wet trunk of a fallen tree, high above the murky bottom. By the time we returned to the selected spot, it was getting dark, and we worked fast to inflate our sleeping mats and spread our bedrolls in the few flat spots we could find among the reeds, rocks, and puddles.

Lightning flickered all around with its accompanying smell of ozone, and the approaching thunder indicated a storm was brewing rapidly. Pierre looked up at the sky thoughtfully and then stated quietly that to remain would be hazardous because the water in the small stream would rise, engulfing us all. We quickly packed up and headed back in the darkening gloom with headlamps attached to our foreheads, the beams splaying this way and that as we slipped and struggled along the now obscure trail. Clutching my bedroll, I negotiated a log crossing the ravine as the rain splashed on the topmost branches of the forest canopy. I have no idea how I made it across, but somehow we all managed without falling off. In one of the other narrow ravines, I was not so lucky. I slipped as I was climbing down and grabbed for a branch that held, but in the process seriously wrenched my back while knocking all the wind out of myself. At the time I remember thinking I was in deep trouble but felt relieved when after a moment I could breathe normally again and my back calmed down to a dull ache.

Back at the compound, we gathered in the hut, dried off, and set up for the ayahuasca ceremony while the skies opened up to a glory of lightning and thunder.

I have never seen a deluge so heavy. Never have I heard rain so loud, nor experienced the waves of moisture crashing through the jungle like they did that night. The monsoon drove down in sheets for hours upon hours, roaring in a rising and falling cadence with the winds that drove it, flying, thundering, shredding the jungle.

The palm frond roof of the hut had been made so expertly, it leaked not even a little, yet it allowed some welcome cooling moisture to come in from the open sides. We partook of the sweet-bitter ayahuasca and settled down to ponder. Listening to the percussion of the drops on the huge leaves of the jungle plants all around, smelling the damp humus of the soaked jungle floor, hypnotically I went deep within. Before long visions came, bringing with them their own tumult, and my awareness of the storm receded into the background, a dramatic symphony playing in concert to an inner landscape. Hours later as the strength of the visions lessened, I became aware of a new sound, an ominous roar coming from below that appeared to be getting nearer and nearer. The small river fifty yards below was no longer small or far away. It had swelled with the rain to a raging torrent, and the banks were now close to the hut.

After we closed the ceremony, some of us stumbled and splashed down to the river, ponchos glistening and spattering in the misty wagging beams of our headlamps, to see what we could. The beautiful stream of clear azure water had transformed into a boiling, mud-brown flood racing at high speed and topping its banks, sending up a fragrance of damp plant matter. A short walk around the corner revealed that the placid pool where we had waded and swum earlier that day no longer existed. The beautiful waterfall cascading into the pond had grown to twenty times its size, the roar of the plunging cataract a truly awesome spectacle to behold. I spent much of what remained of the night mesmerized by nature's dramatic gift.

The next morning as I again sat gazing at the unrelenting flood, I reflected on what might have happened had we remained in the alternative ceremonial spot we had abandoned at the last minute. Surely we would have been swept away to our deaths, on ayahuasca no less. I wondered how many times this had happened to other hapless travelers who, lost in the visions of plant medicines, had been accosted and drowned by a flood.

After the storm, the brown runoff raged for a couple of days until the stream receded back to its pre-storm level. Gone was the lashed wooden raft we had used to float in the pond below the waterfall. The sandbanks and holes were rearranged, as were the damp heaps of logs and debris that choked the stream at intervals. The water had now returned to its exquisite turquoise color, and a warm steam arose from the rock ledges below the falls. On these ledges there arrived a collection of the most beautiful and colorful butterflies I have ever seen. They ranged in size from tiny to so big that their wings were the size of slices of bread. Together they twirled and floated like whirlwinds around little puddles of water. I watched them for hours.

There was a young Peruvian mestizo who with Pierre's per-mission had joined our group on this diet. Rodrigo Maestas (not his real name) was extraordinarily handsome and expressive, with the kind of charm one would expect in a politician. When he threw his head back and laughed, he revealed a full set of even white teeth set against his dark skin and jet-black hair. As Rodrigo talked, his face lit up with animation and his eyes danced, Spanish flowing fluently from his lips. Clearly he was a gifted storyteller and a comedian of sorts. He was a flashy dresser, and on his wrist I was surprised to see a Rolex watch. I wondered how a Peruvian man of his age could come upon such fancy items. Usually young Peruvian men were poor or had modest incomes.

I learned that Rodrigo had been working as an ayahuasquero in northeastern Peru for a number of years, one of the top men at a clinic where ayahuasca was given to alcoholics and cocaine addicts to help them combat their addictions. The clinic was experimental and had been given approval from the govern-ment because it was so successful in producing results. Rodrigo had been asked to leave under a dark cloud of conflict. Later I learned that he had walked off with fifty thousand dollars of the center's money—no wonder he could afford a Rolex. Pierre told me that Rodrigo had come to do some healing work on himself during the diet. He also let me know that Rodrigo was interested in coming to work with him.

For some reason I had a sinking feeling when he told me this. I couldn't imagine Pierre working closely with Rodrigo. This feeling of unease persisted and grew stronger as the days went by. I noticed that Rodrigo loved to be the center of attention and that he would take any opportunity to grab the conversation and focus it on himself. When the topic veered away from him, he would appear to sulk and then leave.

In the group setting around meals, Rodrigo appeared friendly and amiable, but outside when I passed him he took on a different demeanor entirely. He always averted his eyes and never said hello or smiled. I wondered why he did not seem to like me or if I had inadvertently done something to offend him. I tried to smile and say hello in Spanish but he would not respond to me. I began to avoid passing him, and when I saw him coming I would change my direction and take a different route. I found myself feeling resentful that he was on this trip and that I had to deal with him when there was so much internal processing I needed and wanted to do.

At first I chalked up my feelings of being ill at ease to a simple personality conflict. I tend toward introversion, and Rodrigo was clearly an extrovert. I told myself that maybe I was being too judgmental or critical, and I didn't mention my feelings to anyone else because I was somewhat ashamed of my own reaction. Yet little comments others made gave me a sense that they were having difficulty with him as well. Finally, being circumspect and trying to be as neutral as possible, I asked several of the group members if they had any reaction to Rodrigo. They confirmed my suspicions, and Jim, an older man, revealed some information that I did not know. He told me that he had met Rodrigo on one prior occasion in the United States and did not have a favorable impression of him. Rodrigo had come to the United States several years earlier to conduct ceremonies as an ayahuasquero. Reports had it that Rodrigo had been drunk during the ceremonies and ended up hustling all the women. Unfortunately this was not an unusual event among Peruvian ayahuasqeros.

Jim went on to inform me that he had spoken with Pierre at length about Rodrigo and had learned a great deal more. Apparently, Rodrigo had run crosswise with his superior at the clinic where he worked. Although no one knew the details yet, Rodrigo had been asked to leave, partly because he wanted to do things his own way and was no longer following instructions.

He had come to Pierre ostensibly to do a diet and get back on track, but his real agenda was clear. He wanted to work with Pierre to replace the job he had just lost. Pierre had allowed him to come for a couple of reasons. First, Pierre was good-hearted and did not want to refuse to help a man who said he wanted to work on himself. The second reason, however, was more sinister. If he refused, Rodrigo would most likely turn against him and become a problem for him.

Pierre had spoken to us about the intense conflicts, jealousies, and rivalries that are constant in the Amazon area. Shamans were always dueling and sending curses to try to unseat each other. In a way this had value, he said, because it forced you to become strong and learn adequate protection. If you were easily defeated, perhaps you were not strong enough to be a good shaman and healer. Although Pierre never practiced witchcraft himself, he was well aware when it was practiced against him. He said he was constantly dealing with it in one way or another.

Two months earlier he had been riding his motorcycle down the potholed highway running between Iquitos and an outlying town when a giant wasp flew into his mouth and stung him on the inside of his cheek. It practically caused him to crash the bike. Fortunately he retained control of the bike—he could have been killed if he hadn't—but the sting was severe and his mouth and throat swelled up badly. Although he had been treating it, the sting still caused his whole jaw a lot of pain. Pierre was clear the event was a product of sorcery against him. I asked him if it could simply have been an accident, and he told me that in another region of the world it might be, but in the Amazon one had to look at accidents much more carefully.

So Pierre had allowed Rodrigo to come on this trip to keep an eye on him; sometimes it is better to be up close and familiar with a potential enemy than for them to be obscure. Upon reflecting on this, I realized how much strategy and political maneuvering played out in shamans' dealings with one another. Warfare was a reality among them, and only the smartest and savviest could survive. I also realized that Rodrigo's presence posed a potential threat to me as well as my companions. I now knew that I would not have my fantasy of a nice safe trip to the jungle to work with ayahuasca. I would have to deal with not only a difficult person but someone who practiced the negative ways of power and clearly did not like me. The feeling was mutual.

Later I realized he felt competitive with me because I was the designated trip leader for our group, and any competition for attention annoyed him.

I tried to steer clear of him as much as possible but in such a small group this was impossible, especially around mealtimes. I spent some time preoccupied and worried about this state of affairs.

On the second day, we participated in our second ayahuasca ceremony. I deliberately chose a spot in the small ceremonial hut that was at the opposite end from where Rodrigo would be. I could not imagine being on ayahuasca and sitting next to someone I did not like, much less trust. During the ceremony that ensued, Pierre and Don Niko did the lion's share of singing and healing, but on several occasions Rodrigo sang icaros too. His voice was beautiful and full as his songs carried out over the night jungle and the whoosh of the stream below. He seemed to have had some training as a singer. While his songs were pleasant and I could not deny that his voice was wonderful, I felt something important was missing. When Pierre and Don Niko sang, although their voices were not quite as good as Rodrigo's, their songs were powerful and effective. I could feel the effects in my body and in the quality of the visions. When Rodrigo sang, I felt nothing. Perhaps it was my resistance to him, but I came to the conclusion that when he sang, he wanted to entertain rather than heal. I almost felt like he expected us to applaud after each song. He certainly wanted our approval.

After the first several hours when the intensity of the aya-huasca had worn off, we gathered around to share our experiences. When it was my turn, I shared that I had been contemplating why I had become so sick with vomiting and diarrhea before first arriving. I felt I had picked up a lot of static from my many therapy clients and had needed to get rid of that before embark-ing on the weeklong diet. To my shock and surprise, Rodrigo retorted loudly that it was all in my head and that if I didn't want to get sick I did not have to. He implied that I was weak and misled. Still on the effects of the ayahuasca, I felt stung and attacked. Pierre responded at that point, saying that my assess-ment of the situation was accurate and that I needed to learn more about how to protect myself when doing my work. I felt comforted and helped by what he said. Yet I also realized that all the things I had been feeling about Rodrigo were real and that he could be truly vicious.

The next day I spent time lazing in a brightly colored ham-mock stretched between two enormous trees. I draped some mosquito netting over myself and drifted in and out of light dreaming, accompanied by the rush of the river down below. I began to go over the events of the night before, and I had a num-ber of realizations. I knew it was no accident that Rodrigo was here on this diet and I had to deal with him in the most intense of experiences. "Why?" I asked the spirit of ayahuasca, and the response came from the voice of the plant spirit deep within:

Because you desired to evolve and grow and bid for a higher level of personal power in your life. Did you really think that growth would come without a price? When you want to grow at an accelerated pace, you bring up challenges to face, deal with, overcome, and test yourself against. This is no different from desiring to be a better skier. You give yourself ever more challenging hills to come down so your skills will grow. If you always stay on the bunny hill you won't evolve as a skier. If you handle the challenges well, the process can be more enjoyable as well as empowering. The key is not to resist. Know that Rodrigo can't harm you if you don't believe he can. All he can do is bruise your ego if you let him. He is here to deal with his own demons and to give you and others a challenge. Don't resist and he will sink or swim on his own merits.

Upon hearing this I breathed a huge sigh of relief, and tears came to my eyes. Now I had the proper tools to deal with Rodrigo and my disappointment that he was ruining my experience. He could not and would not ruin it if I approached this whole matter from a different point of view. No longer was I a victim of circumstances. Now the question became, "How do I overcome my fear of and resistance to him?" The answer was immediate. "Observe yourself with a sense of humor. If you are too serious, you will fail. If you don't take this seriously enough, you are also finished. The key is to keep your eyes open. Be conscious. Be aware. Be amused. Be free." Although I did not understand all the ramifications of this reply, I got the basic idea. Silently I thanked the ayahuasca spirit for the sage advice. I already felt much more empowered and less obsessed by how to deal with Rodrigo.

From this moment on, I truly was no longer afraid of Rodrigo, nor did I feel his intrusiveness very much. I did observe him and my own reactions to him. I began to see him as a lost and sad little boy who had gotten hold of some toys that he was not old enough for and should not have. Sooner or later he would burn himself, and in fact it appeared that he already had.

Over the next several days I noticed that Pierre took the time to talk with him at great length. I did not know what they were saying but later I found out that Pierre was trying to get him to be honest and set him on a better course—as it turned out, to no avail. Later I took a walk in the forest outside of camp and saw Rodrigo talking with Don Niko. Don Niko came to Pierre afterward with the news that Rodrigo was putting Pierre down and trying to get Don Niko to go over to his side and start a botanical garden and diet outpost to compete with Pierre's. Apparently, Rodrigo was scathing in his judgment that Pierre was working with gringos and making money off them, and he was trying to use this as the reason for Don Niko to abandon Pierre. Don Niko, being faithful to Pierre, would have none of it.

Although Pierre told me nothing about all of this, I shared with him that I distrusted Rodrigo. I'm sure he did not need to hear it, but I wanted Pierre to have independent observations about the kind of person Rodrigo was: a treacherous, sneaky, and undermining person who could cause no end of difficulty if allowed to.

Through this experience, I was once again reminded that to be an ayahuasquero or curandero is no simple matter. You have to be a good psychologist and highly attentive at all times to handle difficult personalities who might not have your best interests in mind. I admired Pierre's fortitude because not only was he responsible for the well-being of all of us throughout the diet, but he had to contend with additional burdens as well. He exhibited a great deal of patience and I never saw him angry. He seemed always to keep the welfare of the others foremost in his mind, including that of someone who was attempting to undermine him.

One day I decided to take a walk in the jungle and followed a trail that Pierre had indicated would take me to a pool a couple of miles distant. I needed a little alone time and some exercise to stretch my legs and enjoy the jungle. Quickly I left the encampment behind and followed a fairly well cut out trail through pristine virgin jungle with ayahuasca vines bigger than whole tree trunks climbing high into the canopy to hang from massive trees.

After about half an hour of walking, I had the strange feeling that I was not alone. I heard snuffling sounds on both sides of the trail. I stopped and cocked my head to listen but there was no more noise, so I cautiously forged ahead, coming to a muddy place dug up by hooved feet. I noticed big patches of a white mineral substance on the ground. Then the snuffling came back—on all sides of me, now much louder and more active. In the underbrush I spotted a huge peccary (a piglike mammal), then another, and still another. As I looked around, I saw many peccaries surrounding me, all watching me with their squinty eyes.

In that moment I remembered a story Pierre had told me. Several of his friends were hiking through the jungle accompanied by their large dog. They came upon a big herd of peccaries and, realizing the danger, climbed trees to get out of range of the creatures' jaws. Only the large dog, who could not climb, was left. By the time the peccaries got through with the dog, there was not a hair left of him. When the peccaries left, the men climbed down and made their escape.

Running would be catastrophic and there were no trees I could climb easily, so I very slowly reached into my pocket and pulled out my pouch of tobacco and my wooden jungle pipe with the carved monkey face that Pierre had given me as a ceremonial tool. I filled the pipe and began to smoke it, giving an offering of tobacco to the peccaries. I also said some very earnest prayers to Spirit to get me out of there safely. Slooooowwwly I went back the way I had come, blowing out clouds of tobacco smoke. The peccaries watched me intently but made no move toward me. When I got out of their range, I walked swiftly back to camp, realizing that I had walked into a salt lick where they had all been gathering. Perhaps they were more interested in the salt than me, or perhaps the tobacco offering worked better than I imagined. Whatever the case, I lived to tell the tale to my group. Pierre noted it was an encounter with power that I navigated well. I did discover that I had accumulated some power by facing off the peccaries. Did the peccaries have anything to do with Rodrigo? Was this salt lick with accompanying dangerous peccaries symbolic of dealing with Rodrigo? Perhaps! If so, I was learning to handle it with a better outcome.

On the third night of ceremony, we gathered in the evening to partake of the ayahuasca tea and repeat our prayers for visions and healing. After a couple of hours the visions were coming strong and the jungle remained black as pitch, creating a perfect backdrop for the brilliant landscapes welling up from within. Then, without warning, there was a sudden earsplitting explosion, like the sound of a shotgun, from ten feet away. In the middle of ayahuasca visions, I was unprepared for such a loud noise and not exactly in a rational state of mind to respond adequately. I had the thought that our hunter's gun had accidently gone off, and I wondered if anyone had been hit. I could not quite fathom anyone attacking us in so remote a place. I heard people getting up and moving around. I heard the garbled voice of Pierre talking in hushed tones to Don Niko. Feeling that I had to know what happened, I crawled over to Pierre and asked him what the noise was. He told me that one of the glass bottles of ayahuasca had exploded and shattered due to fermentation but that luckily it was inside his colorful cotton bag, so the glass was contained. I went back to my spot clearer about what had happened but uneasy about its meaning. Was the spirit of ayahuasca trying to tell us something? Were we doing something wrong? Was Rodrigo's energy responsible for this near disaster? My visions were interrupted, and for the rest of the evening I could never quite get back to where I had been. I could not feel the strength of the medicine and felt some disappointment.

The next day we discussed the exploding bottle incident. Pierre seemed to feel that it was a good sign suggesting that the medicine was very strong and potent. Although I trusted him and valued his opinion, I had a hard time agreeing with his evaluation. I had a sense of foreboding and felt ill at ease. The situation with Rodrigo was becoming explosive.

That evening we gathered in the hut for another round of ayahuasca tea and took up our stations around the central altar where Pierre and Don Niko presided. I decided to shift my position from the other nights because I wanted a new perspective. I chose to rest my back against a support pole and use my stuffed lightweight sleeping bag as a cushion for my back.

The ceremony went well. Afterward, in the wee hours of the morning as I groped for my toothbrush, a large brown jungle spider as big around as the palm of my hand emerged from my toiletries bag and scrambled through the floorboards of the hut, freaking me out rather badly. Of all the creatures on earth, spiders have always been the ones that I can be phobic about.

I soon realized that the spider had quickly crawled away without harming me. Then in the light of my headlamp I saw several flying insects clinging to the inside of my mosquito net. Their shadows from the beam of my light were eerily huge on the top of the hut. I counted three of them and saw that they were wasps. Suddenly there were four, then five, then eight, then fifteen. The air in the mosquito net was rapidly filling with angry buzzing wasps. Still under the influence of ayahuasca, I had to ask myself if they were real or some nightmare from my subconscious.

As I started to get into my sleeping bag, I felt a needle-sharp pain in my hand and realized that the wasps were quite real and deadly. The pain shot up my arm as I was stung again and then again. I pulled back the bag and there inside was a whole nest of swarming, buzzing wasps.

Trying to move as gingerly as possible, I crawled out from under the mosquito net while some of the wasps escaped from it too and buzzed around my head. I realized that I needed help, and at the same time I heard someone mumble in a drowsy voice, "What's going on?" I cried desperately, "I need some help! A swarm of wasps is attacking me!" In that moment I was sure the group would think I had lost it and succumbed to some psychotic delusion under the influence of ayahuasca. Jim hesitated only a moment and then crawled out to help me. Together we carried the mosquito net and the bag out to the jungle on sticks. But I needed the net to protect me from mosquitos, so we had to clean it out. Swatting and waving our arms while trying to hold the sticks, for over an hour we struggled with the dilemma of the wasps. I flung the sleeping bag out into the jungle darkness, and we concentrated on clearing out the net. We managed to clear away the wasps but Jim was stung a couple of times. Exhausted, I profusely thanked him, and once again set up the net to try to sleep out the rest of the night. It was now about four thirty in the morning and the light of dawn would be arriving soon. As I lay back down on my pad feeling the ache from the wasp stings, my mind wandered to fearful thoughts about the consequences of being stung while on ayahuasca: the venom mixed with aya-huasca might poison me. It could stop my heart at any minute, or it could cause me to be unable to breathe.

I remembered a story Pierre had told me about a particularly dangerous wasp whose sting was devastating to humans and other animals. As it stung, it would lay some eggs under the skin. Before long the skin would swell and fester, a red ring would grow around the sting, and the flesh would putrefy. Eventually this process would spread to all parts of the body and become fatal. There was no simple cure. Unfortunate people so afflicted would be shot full of some highly toxic metallic substance that, it was hoped, would retard the destructive spread of the wasp sting and the buried eggs.

I realized I must put aside these thoughts as best I could, knowing that the situation was insoluble at the moment and only time would tell the outcome. Sleep abandoned me and I contemplated what the attack meant: the appearance of the spider, the nest of wasps in my sleeping bag, and the stinging. Was the jungle trying to chase me out? Was it another sign that I was not ready for this experience? Had I offended the spirit of ayahuasca in some way? Was I being cursed by Rodrigo, the dark shaman? Finding no clear answers, I listened to the sounds of the jungle as dawn slowly broke over the Amazon.

After breakfast and tending to the wasp stings, I decided I had better deal with the wasps in my sleeping bag. I carefully retrieved the bag where it lay, draped over a bush. As I came closer I noticed a mass of movement in and around the bag. Millions of small ants were snaking up the trunk of the bush and into the bag. As I pulled back the folds of the green sleeping bag, my eyes beheld an amazing sight. The ants were attacking the wasps, biting them into parts and carrying them away piece by piece. I watched fascinated that such small creatures could overcome insects that had given me, so much larger, such a problem. The wasps could not use their stingers on the small ants, and for some reason the wasps did not fly off but resigned themselves to the fate of being dismantled and carried off.

After watching for a time, I realized that it was best to let the ants do their work; I would come back later to deal with the ant problem. When I returned many hours later, I found the bag impeccably clean and empty—there was no sign of ants, wasps, or any of the drama I had witnessed. I marveled at what an efficient ecosystem existed in this forested part of the world.

Later I contemplated these events from the hammock, my daily napping spot overlooking the river and the falls. I understood that the spider and the wasps represented my fears made manifest. I saw that in such intense circumstances, feelings could actually precipitate events in the world to mirror the interior landscape. The spider startled me but did not harm me. The wasps stung me, but I was not injured in the long run. The ants cleaned up the mess, and this mirrored my internal world. I mused about the small size of the industrious ants and how thoroughly they had done their job. If the wasps represented my fears, the ants must represent the resources I owned for handling my fears. In the end there was no sign of spider, ants, or wasps. There was also no sign of my fear other than a reminder in the form of some red spots on my skin.

Upon reflection I realized that when I had draped the sleeping bag over a roof support earlier and left it to dry, a hive of wasps had found it attractive as a house. When I stuffed the bag, they were all inside and I did not see them, and when I attempted to get into the bag, they all flew out, angry at having been confined so tightly for so long. Perhaps there was a part of me that had been confined too long that sought expression. When it finally came out, it raised a little fury and then was no longer viable. Something very small handled it completely.

In the final ceremony I had a very bad feeling about Pierre. Under the influence of ayahuasca, I saw that someone or a group of individuals was going to try to kill him. Rodrigo? I suspected him. I couldn't shake the dark feeling no matter what I tried to do—there is nothing quite so dark as an ayahuasca ceremony that goes negative. In the morning as the sun rose and lit up the jungle, it still looked unnervingly dark to me. I felt some kind of evil everywhere around me, although I knew it wasn't mine and had nothing to do with me. I confided all this to Pierre and told him I was very concerned for him. I had no evidence, only what the ayahuasca had shown me. He listened intently and, uncharacteristically, said he saw it too.

◻

When Pierre and our group returned to his compound in Iquitos after the diet, I lingered for a couple of days to recover and rest. We were sitting around the dining table at his botanical gardens after a particularly enjoyable meal. As usual I was pressing Pierre for more stories about his life in the Amazon before founding his gardens; being in a loquacious mood, he was glad to oblige. Pierre told a tale about his experiences working as a curandero visiting remote villages where there were no doctors or medical facilities. A number of years back he was in a distant village that was also being visited by two of the ever-intrusive fundamentalist Christian missionaries who frequented the backwaters of the Amazon. Pierre explained that there was no love lost between missionaries and a traditional curandero. In fact, missionaries sought to get rid of them in every way possible. So there was an uneasy tension in the village between them. Pierre went on to recount what happened.

A father went fishing with his six-year-old son on a sandy beach of the nearby river. The father decided to try another spot a little further down the beach where the fishing might be better. He instructed his son to remain where he was and to continue playing in the sand. While the father fished, a deadly poisonous snake slithered onto the beach and struck the boy. When the fisherman returned, he found the boy unconscious on the beach, overcome by the snakebite but still breathing shallowly. He put the boy in the dugout and paddled as fast as he could back to the village, where he ran carrying the boy and shouting for help.

Pierre, hearing the cries, rushed out and helped carry the boy inside a hut and laid him out on a mat. Pierre immediately applied emergency treatment to the boy's wound and took measures to bring the fever under control. He then instructed the father and the other villagers to stand guard and watch the boy for the next couple of days. He said the boy had a good chance of recovery but that they should under no circumstances give him any water. In a snakebite situation you must deprive the person of water for some hours immediately after the bite or they will die. If they drink, the fluid will hydrate the flesh and help carry the poison to all parts of the body. Depriving the person of fluids keeps the poison localized where it can do less damage.

Pierre told the villagers that the boy would wake up with a terrible thirst but that they would have to withstand his cries until the danger had passed. Pierre's services were needed elsewhere and he could not stay with the boy, though he said he would come back soon to check on him. Sure enough, after Pierre left, the boy awoke with a terrific thirst.

The missionaries staying at the village could not wait for Pierre to leave. Not wanting to be upstaged by this non-Christian curandero, they said that his instruction to deprive the boy of water was superstitious claptrap designed to keep a hold on the villagers. Secretly, of course, they believed that Pierre's presence was making their missionary work harder.

When the boy began to cry for water, one of the missionaries brought a Coke to give him. But the villagers protested, and there was a standoff. The missionaries then said they would watch the boy for a while and sure enough, when no one else was there to stop them, they gave the boy the cola. He died within the hour.

When the boy's father and the villagers discovered he was dead, there was a great commotion. The missionaries, fearing for their lives, blamed the death on Pierre, saying he had worked some evil magic that killed the boy. They managed to convince some villagers of this and created enough doubt among them that they were off the hook. When Pierre returned the next morning, a villager who was loyal to him met him at the edge of the village. He explained what had happened and told Pierre that he must leave at once because some of the villagers were planning to kill him. Pierre had no choice but to flee for his life.

We were mesmerized by his storytelling in the flickering candlelight. We were silent and horrified when he finished. From this tragic tale I realized that there is a harsh and brutal side to life in the Amazon that cannot be understood from the perspective of a simple tourist. I also began to understand that nasty politics play a role even in the most remote locales. Pierre went on to tell us that this was by no means an isolated incident. Many healers and curanderos have been run off and even killed by the machinations of the missionaries over the years.

The night was still young so we asked Pierre if he could tell us another story about life in the jungle. He thought a moment and then chuckled heartily. "This night seems to be about snakes," he said. "I'll tell you another one about a snakebite but this one is very different in nature." Pierre explained that a number of years ago he was visiting villages in an area he did not know well. He had to be very careful in some areas because if you don't know the local customs you can get yourself in big trouble in a hurry; under those circumstances he usually observed for a while before offering to help. One day a man was bitten by a poisonous snake, and a friend came to the edge of the village to ask for help. The village elders met and refused to allow the man into the village because if he died there, they might be plagued by his ghost. After some wrangling, it was decided that the man would be brought to a hut just outside the village where he could be treated.

Pierre noted that they gave instructions not to give the man any water or fluids. The man, feeling a fiery thirst, cried out for water and they refused him. After about twenty-four hours the man continued to plead for fluids but the elders of the village ordered that none be given him. Pierre began to feel concern because by now the snakebite victim was beyond the danger point and could be given fluids.

Time passed and the elders continued their order to refuse the man any food or water. The man was now beginning to show signs of dehydration, and his cries were weaker. Pierre did not know what to do. He felt the man needed water but did not know the local customs of the village and did not understand why the elders were refusing the man water. Three days came and went and still water was refused the man. Pierre did not want to cross the elders because this could prove fatal to himself, and he thought that maybe they had knowledge that he did not have in this situation.

After four days without water, the man expired. Nobody grieved. Pierre was horrified. Then the elders explained to him why they had taken this action. The man who had been bitten by the snake was a village troublemaker. He drank too much, stole things from the other villagers, and had a history of violent behavior toward others, including his wife and children. In the past he had killed other members of the village in drunken fights. No one liked him. The elders decided that the snake-bite was a kind of punishment for his misdeeds. He was refused water as a way of executing him. What Pierre had witnessed was an example of jungle justice.

○

Weeks later, after I had returned to Santa Fe, I heard that Pierre had abandoned the beautiful outpost at Regalia after receiving anonymous death threats. A short time later he left Peru altogether under threats to his life. That is how it came to pass that I had to stop working with Pierre and began searching for other teachers.

Rodrigo surfaced in the United States again. He became a well-known and popular ayahuasqero, making his way into conferences, conventions, and the media. He gained many followers and wrote a book about himself. I tried to warn a person

I respected who was sponsoring him, but he did not want to hear me. Rodrigo was very charming, but he became careless, drew too much attention to himself, and suffered serious consequences for it. That is all I will say about the matter. He apparently has more lessons to learn.

POSTSCRIPT

Sometimes an encounter with power comes in the form of a serious challenge, a confrontation with the dark side, a threat to safety and comfort. You do not become more powerful by remaining in your comfort zone: the price of power is your own comfort. Blaming, resisting, judging, whining, and feeling like a victim are not the ways of power, but the ways to lose the opportunity to become more powerful. To become more powerful you must be vulnerable—but not stupid. Neutrality is a strong stance, the best stance, because it allows you to observe without resistance. Self-observation is a royal road to more power, for through observing comes much critical information that can lead to wisdom. Another staple of power is forgiveness, the ability to see with compassion and insight. Although Rodrigo was acting without integrity, even dangerously, he was coming from a place of insecurity, a deeply fearful child pursuing glitter on the outside but on the run on the inside.

Safety is to be found within. Someone can attack you verbally but you can choose whether to be hurt. People exploring the darkness of fear can hurt you only if you agree to be hurt.

Explosive events often coincide with explosive emotions in explosive situations. Nothing is isolated from everything else. Everything is interwoven and explored by essence. In this sense there are no accidents.

QUESTIONS

At times we can be living in a dangerous world. Can you forgive someone who is currently attacking you, emotionally or otherwise, who may in fact be dangerous to you? What are your options? Where are your boundaries and how can you set them?

13

AN ENCOUNTER WITH THE DOLPHIN BRUJOS

The cool reddish-brown water swirled all around me as I looked up at a peerless blue sky, white billowy storm clouds rising in the heat of the Amazon basin. A spectacular double rainbow arched across the sky, brilliant in its palette of exquisite colors, and I wondered if anything could quite match this outrageous display. I looked around for the boat carrying the rest of our party and found it behind me, starkly silhouetted against the reddening sky in the west. It was getting late but this was just too good to pass up: a swim with a pod of the famous pink river dolphins arcing out of the water all around us.

Suddenly I felt a hard bump on my thigh, obviously not one of the little fish skimming over my body and feeding on dead skin, but a more substantial creature. I heard my daughter, Anna, swimming nearby give a little cry as she, too, got a hard bump. There were several other people in the water as well, but only Lena, Anna, and I reported the bumps. It seemed to be a family affair.

Minutes later, I was crawling on board the boat, a difficult task since there was no ladder and it required hauling myself aboard by sheer strength. As I strained to climb on I felt a muscle pull in my back. The boat rocked from the turbulence created at the confluence of the Ucayali and Marañón rivers. Here, these vast rivers in Peru come together to form the Amazon River, the longest river in the world. As the boat headed back upstream along the Ucayali, I glanced at the sky and realized we were probably not going to make it back to our camp before dark. We were with our two-year study group who called themselves the Owls, and true to form we always ended up finishing our excursions in the dark. It became a kind of inside joke. To my knowledge none of us had brought flashlights or headlamps, although we should have. Sunset in the Amazon is a rapid affair because the sun goes straight down and darkness falls fast. Upstream, dark storm clouds revealed a curtain of rain rapidly approaching us. In moments we were inundated, and the boat was forced to pull off to the bank and wait out the deluge, a typical occurrence here in the jungle but one that lost us precious daylight. The rainy season was usually over by now, but this year it was lingering and everything on land was extremely muddy. Darkness soon fell, but someone in our party had brought a headlamp, a stroke of good fortune because it guided us to shore.

With only a wee bit of light, we slid and stumbled back to our camp in Yarapa in our rain boots as clouds of mosquitos found and feasted on us. By this time my lower back was killing me and I realized I had seriously pulled something getting into the boat. I was in an amazing amount of pain. In one hour we planned to begin an intense ceremony with plant medicines, the third of four ceremonies in five nights. We had arrived in this remote area with our two-year shamanic study group to work with Enrique, Herlinda, and their assistant and son-in-law, Davide, whom we had imported to this non-Shipibo area of the jungle. There were twenty-two of us inside a big, beautiful maloka, a round ceremonial hut designed for such use. I rigged up a hammock because my back hurt a lot and I knew I could not sit on the floor all night. We took the medicine and shortly I realized what had happened in the river that afternoon. We'd had an encounter with *brujos* (sorcerers), the pink river dolphins of lore.

Now, you are probably wondering how a cute pink river dolphin could possibly be a sorcerer and that is what I thought too, something that led me to be very careless. In the Amazon, the pink river dolphins that tourists love to see are both revered and feared by the indigenous people who live along the river and fish its waters. There are many stories about young women having to be careful because the male dolphins occasionally come ashore and have their way with them. The older shamans all say that in the old days their ancestors used to go underwater to visit the dolphins and learn from their vast store of knowledge and power. Sometimes the human shamans would be gone for many days in the watery kingdom, learning to breathe underwater and navigate its vast reaches.

Paintings and artistic renderings of the Amazon region show pink dolphins with the bodies of men and the heads of dolphins conducting ceremonies and offering healings. I always thought this was mythology, the superstition of the jungle. Little did I realize what they were referring to until that day on the river and that night in ceremony.

When we arrived at the confluence of the rivers earlier that day to see the pink dolphins, we spotted a whole pod swimming all around us. I distinctly heard the call in my mind to take my clothes off and jump in the water with them, and I immediately did. However, only a few in our party followed my lead. Enrique, Herlinda, and Davide did not enter the water. They seemed to be concerned rather than lighthearted, as they usually were. But I failed to notice because I was having too much fun and was distracted by the sights and sounds of the river, the rainbows, the clouds, and the dolphins.

That evening as the medicine started taking effect, I began to feel the dolphins' presence within me and it was quite overwhelming. I felt their power and the depth of their world, and I knew beyond a shadow of a doubt that they were sorcerers and that I had strayed into their world and their influence. This perception terrified me. I did not feel their cuteness or their friendliness, but their raw power, as if I had just met Carlos Castaneda's teacher, Don Juan Matus, and failed one of his tests.

During the ceremony that night I crawled over to where Enrique was sitting and spoke to him about my experience. In the dark I could feel him laughing at me and at the same time expressing concern for my difficulty. He told me that I had endangered myself by jumping into the water because the pink dolphins were very powerful and masters of their underwater world. He said he could see that I had not asked permission to enter the water. I explained to him that I had felt their call and responded to it by entering the water. He laughed and said the dolphins were known as tricksters and they just wanted to test me to see if I would ask permission after being called. Since I didn't, they came up and struck me in the water, as they did Anna and Lena. That blow, Enrique said, was a jolt of energy that would go in the direction I aimed it. Another test! If I had been more prepared, I could have used that jolt for greater power. Instead, I allowed it to create pain in my body, which I then blamed on them. This was foolish and was a good representation of what we all do when we do not take responsibility for our actions.

So as the power of the evening ceremony unfolded, I was first outraged. I felt the dolphins had tricked and then harmed me because I made an innocent mistake. The more I thought about it, though, the more I realized that they had done nothing harmful to me. They merely tested me and gave me the opportunity to hang myself or not. I saw that if I had any false personality, arrogance, martyrdom, or impatience, they would activate it and throw it in my face. I learned the hard way, but rapidly. I realized the dolphins could be very powerful teachers, though I was not free to work with them because I was working with other teachers, Enrique and Herlinda.

Enrique helped me that evening by singing a long song to the dolphins asking their forgiveness for my foolishness in entering their domain without permission. He then removed all their influence over me, which left me with mixed feelings. I had failed a test, but at the same time I had learned something very valuable. I flirted with power and managed to survive it, but according to Enrique the dolphins' influence was incompatible with the songs and patterns that the Shipibos had been putting in my energy body all week. He told me the dolphins used water songs and the Shipibos used plant songs and I could not work with them both at the same time. That both relieved me and made me feel a little sad.

Later Herlinda told me that she avoided the dolphins because, while they are very powerful, their trickster teaching style made her feel uncomfortable. I have to admit that I felt the same. The trickster style leads to fast learning, but you have to have a pretty thick skin to tolerate it. I respond better to a respectful, loving style.

Lena said the dolphins showed her their mastery over the water systems of the world. They told her that all water is connected everywhere and because they live so intimately in their watery environment, they know exactly what is going on in all parts of the world. They revealed to her some of their profound and vast domain and showed her a little of what they know. She was duly impressed but not inclined to follow their brujo-style teaching methods. Being an Aquarian, she had a somewhat more benevolent experience with them.

Enrique later told me that the Shipibo see rainbows as extremely powerful, even dangerous at times, and they are quite careful when rainbows are in the sky. Having a double rainbow while we were in the water with the dolphins meant potentially more power and energy than we could deal with. Yet I was distracted by the beauty and my own silly notions of romantically swimming with the dolphins and failed to sense the power I was fooling with. Another shamanic lesson survived and learned.

POSTSCRIPT

Since this experience, I no longer see dolphins as cute entertainers. I see raw power and have great respect for what they know. That said, not all dolphins are sorcerers and many of them may employ another teaching style. The pink Amazon dolphins are brujos, just as there are certain locales on land where humans are brujos.

Regarding the rainbows, although I can still appreciate their great beauty, I now have much more respect for the power they represent and am much more conscious of my thoughts while a rainbow is visible in the sky. It is not just the Shipibo who regard rainbows as powerful. The Huichol also have great respect for them, and if one appears in the sky they immediately stop everything and pray with bowed heads.

At a recent retreat on our land in New Mexico during a power animal exercise with a large group, I was amazed at how many times dolphins came up as messengers. I realized that they are hanging around and making themselves available as information sources. They are powerful and good allies, but one must be careful in interacting with them. An ally is like a power tool. It can be wonderful and supportive, but it can also hurt you if you don't handle it with care and respect. In the world of shamanism, respect is everything and cuteness is irrelevant, even a distraction.

EXERCISE

Next time you see a rainbow, stop and pay attention. What had you been contemplating just prior to encountering it? What do you need help with at this time? Compliment the great beauty of the rainbow and then put in your request for help. Keep track of what happens.

14

NEVADO ACONCAGUA

Pilgrimage to a Sacred Mountain for Power

Like a faintly remembered dream, the first urgings to climb the highest mountain in the Western Hemisphere kept creeping into the corners of my awareness. *Insanity*, I told myself. Why would a fifty-five-year-old man with a loving family and an interesting profession subject himself to the rigors of climbing a twenty-two-thousand-foot mountain in South America? Why would I double the risk by going with my wife to a mountain known to harbor the littered corpses of international climbers? All of our friends shook their heads and issued dire warnings about such a trip. They gravely issued comments like "I'll be praying for you" and "I just hope you make it back alive." Their concern was authentic but the message was disconcerting. Yet as I discovered, the truth be told, I simply could not *not* go.

It all started in 1989, in Alberta, Canada, when I had the good fortune to meet Laurie Skreslet, a powerhouse of a man with Norwegian ancestry whose grip about broke my hand when he greeted me for the first time. Like chiseled rock, his face meant serious outdoor business, but his smile was warm and genuine, his eyes curious and investigative. I had traveled north to Edmonton to give a lecture and slide show on an ancient system of personality analysis. Laurie had made the long trip from Calgary out of genuine interest.

Laurie knew something about personalities too, but from a totally different context. He was the first Canadian to summit Mount Everest in 1982 and subsequently assisted Sharon Wood in 1986 in becoming the first woman from the Western Hemisphere to summit. He knew about personalities under pressure and character under extreme stress—as well as the lack of maturity and experience as a soul, or essence. As a mountain guide, he wanted to know more about what makes people behave the way they do, especially under extreme conditions.

As we conversed, I soon learned that we also shared a deep interest in shamanism, the ancient nature-based spirituality encountered all over the world and practiced by indigenous peoples on all continents. This common interest forged a long-term relationship that would culminate in the Aconcagua climb.

Laurie was very interested in the fact that Lena and I were offering courses in shamanic studies, and he lost no time in signing up for a seventeen-day course and then a two-year study program. Laurie had done high-altitude climbing in Peru and wanted to understand the mountains he climbed in a deeper way, one that provided self-empowerment and increased self-awareness that he could also impart to his climbing clients and the corporate audiences he spoke to on a regular basis. We found that as we told Laurie about our experiences with shamans and their practices, he inspired us with his knowledge of high-altitude climbing and its similarities to the shamanic approach to life.

He shared with us a striking event that preceded his first successful Everest bid. In Nepal just before the climb, he befriended a Nepalese family who eventually introduced him to a powerful lama of the Tibetan Bonpo tradition, an ancient approach based on shamanic practice that appeared before the introduction of Buddhism in Tibet. The lama looked at him and then divined that the venture to climb Everest would be extremely difficult, fraught with dangers and tragedies, but that Laurie would meet with ultimate success if he made the proper offerings to the mountain, a process the lama outlined carefully. Laurie followed this advice to the letter even though he did not understand any of it at the time. Although there were five deaths in the team's campaign for the summit and Laurie suffered broken ribs trying to retrieve the body of the team photographer from a crevasse, he was the first to make it to the summit. Only one other Canadian climber achieved the summit right after him and he was sensitive to Laurie's offerings. Other members of the team failed to summit and of course they did not follow the same practices he did.

Since the 1980s, Laurie has been leading trips to Mount Aconcagua on the Argentina-Chile border because it offers a number of advantages. The summit can be reached without oxygen, the mountain is relatively easy and inexpensive to access, and there is little jet lag in the travel from North America. Eventually he convinced us that we could make the climb despite our ages and lack of technical prowess. However, we had several false starts. The first year we planned to go, I tore my meniscus and had surgery instead of climbing the mountain. The next year I had a bad feeling about the timing and decided not to go; as it turned out, there were some big problems on that trip and the summit bid had to be aborted. Mount Aconcagua must be climbed during a fairly short window during the summer in the Southern Hemisphere; the time frame is from mid-November through February. Finally, in the early winter of 2003 the time was right.

In preparation for the climb, we needed to get into mountain condition by going for daily strenuous hikes in the Sangre de Cristo Mountains behind Santa Fe. Fortunately they rise to over twelve thousand feet, which allowed for some altitude acclimatization. We also traveled to the Canadian Rockies for a six-day winter trek with all the clients under Laurie's supervision to see if we could cut the mustard on the big mountain to the south. We prepared ourselves mentally and spiritually with daily practices in meditation and chi gong. The way we were thinking of it, this was not going to be an ordinary climb for two middle-aged professionals; rather, it would be a climb utilizing all our abilities, inner and outer, a test of our shamanic training and discipline. This was to be a bid for power, a kind of self-imposed shamanic initiation, a pilgrimage to a sacred mountain. And we needed to be absolutely prepared in every way.

Prior to leaving the United States, we carefully packed and organized enough food for eighteen days on the mountain, with extra days included in case of foul weather. In addition, we needed light but extremely warm clothing, heavy-duty plastic mountain boots, crampons, trekking poles, light but high-volume backpacks, four-season tents, and high-altitude cooking stoves. Despite its great height, Aconcagua, the crown jewel of the Andes, has many routes that can be climbed without technical equipment. Alternatively, routes like the South Face, a massive wall, and the Polish Glacier pose world-class technical challenges complete with crevasses and shifting blocks of ice. We naturally chose a nontechnical route in recognition of our lack of professional expertise.

In Mendoza, an Argentinian city near the mountain, we met our small team. It consisted of Laurie, our principal guide, fifty-four; Bill Marler, forty-nine, an unassuming but exceptionally competent Canadian mountain guide; and three paying clients besides ourselves: Fred, fifty, owner of a U.S. paper company;

and TJ, fifty-two, a Canadian entrepreneur who had attempted three times to climb Aconcagua without success. Kathy, twenty-nine, a physical therapist from the United States, was to meet us in the mountains after a delayed flight. Rounding out the trip were Lena, fifty-one, and me, fifty-five, the "old man" of the trip.

The trip to the starting point takes about three hours, and the ride was spectacular. We stayed at a ski resort near the Chilean border in the nine-thousand-foot range, a funky but passable climbers' lodging. We spent the first day out training and acclimating, and we hiked with daypacks up a beautiful canyon, where we were met by hawks and condors that swooped over the cliffs. We counted six condors, one for each of our team members, and then finally a seventh one arrived to account for our seventh member, Kathy, who was delayed. We all laughed with great amusement and delight at this obvious synchronicity.

There are two main points of entry to Aconcagua and two base camps, one on either side of the mountain. The most popular route leads to the Plaza de Mulas at about thirteen thousand feet, a twenty-five-mile trek up a beautiful valley. This route offers the fastest entry to the mountain but little chance to acclimatize and almost no views of the mountain. Since time is of the essence for most climbers, they prefer this route. But Laurie had abandoned it long ago for two good reasons: he prefers to acclimatize his clients by taking more time to get to base camp, and the other route had become too crowded.

Professional and nonprofessional climbers from all over the world flock to Aconcagua because of its easy access and because it can be climbed nontechnically. As a qualified mountain guide, Laurie told us it was his obligation to help any climbers in trouble, and that doing so can be very distracting from leading his own groups. He took us on the longer and more difficult Polish Glacier traverse route, a four-day trek up the Quebrada de las Vacas (Valley of

Cows) and then up the Quebrada de Rio Linchos. This route can be extraordinarily hot and windy, but we were fortunate to have cool weather despite the intense winds. We learned from early returnees that so far the season had been dangerously cold and windy on the mountain. The week before, a number of expedition tents in base camps were wrecked or flattened by hundred-mile-per-hour winds.

I felt sobered, but Laurie dismissed the reports, saying the weather on the mountain could change at any time and we would deal with the weather we encountered. Since he had gone to the summit more than twenty times and was the expert, I was inclined to take his word for it. Still, I felt intimidated. According to our shamanic training, this would be our first major challenge, facing our fears directly and moving through them without resistance. When you are doing something on the cutting edge of your abilities, making a bid for power, there is always fear to face.

With this in mind we started our trek with a shamanic ceremony of prayers and offerings of tobacco and Agua Florida from Peru. Although our trekking companions were unfamiliar with the shamanic way, they good-naturedly participated. We gave them each an eagle or hawk feather (garnered from the Mendoza zoo) to carry as an offering to the mountain apu and leave at any place they wished.

The walk to base camp took four days, and before too long we were scattered along the trail, leaving us with many hours of solitary walking. Depending on one's temperament, this could be difficult or a welcome opportunity to commune with the mountains. I used the opportunity to listen to nature, watch for animals, and pray to Spirit for a good trip. After navigating the Quebrada de las Vacas, we arrived at the Quebrada de Rio Linchos, where we viewed the mountain in all its glory for the first time, and the stormy weather gave it a somber and stark appearance.

At this juncture I decided to perform a simple tobacco ceremony I had learned from my Andean shaman teachers in Peru. This is to ask permission to approach the apu. A powerful mountain guardian and an elemental spirit who watches over the land for miles around, an apu is considered an intense concentration of power and energy that can be tapped for personal objectives, but it can also be quite dangerous. According to Incan tradition, you must approach it with the utmost respect or it can take your life. The Incas say that the apus come in pairs, one female and one male, and it is best to greet both of them. Aconcagua is no different in that it is flanked to the east by Mount Armandino, a male apu not quite as high. According to an Incan tradition that we learned in Lake Titicaca, the male apu must be approached first. You must then ask permission to approach the female apu, in this case Mount Aconcagua.

Both Laurie and Bill, our second mountain guide, told me that this ceremonial style has always felt to them like the correct way to approach the mountains. Most people, they said, come only to summit and they miss the real meaning of the mountains here: the power, the respect, the gifts they offer. Not only do most climbers overlook these important aspects, but they miss the beauty as well. Many complain that the mountain is ferociously windy and cold and call it a giant slag heap, as if it were unworthy of their efforts to climb it. We conjectured that perhaps according to shamanic tradition, this is why the mountain claims many lives every year.

Laurie invited us to savor the rock formations, the greenery, and the stark beauty of the surrounding peaks on the approach to base camp. We were on the lookout for guanacos, the handsome barking dromedaries of this region that leave crisscrossed trails all over the higher slopes. Laurie helped us find guanaco hollows, dead spots in the wind where the guanacos like to lie down to rest. They are marvelously still places where the cold wind abates completely. He taught us about the importance of not rushing, of taking a slow pace to conserve energy and appreciate what the mountains have to teach. He wanted us to take care of our bodies and acclimatize slowly so they would carry us unfailingly to the highest elevations. He showed us how to feel the power of this soaring land anchoring our slow-moving feet. He demonstrated for us how to walk carefully to reduce fatigue and strain on our tendons and muscles. Every turn of an ankle and slip on a rock could sap energy and fatigue us unnecessarily, he warned. We should pay attention to what our feet were doing to conserve our limited resources. Both he and Bill were filled with the knowledge of many tricks to stay warm and relaxed even in this rugged environment. They extolled us to hydrate often and stop at the first sign of a hot spot on our feet. I was impressed with how tuned in Laurie was to the beauty and nature of this stark and harsh environment. He constantly pointed out natural features that I would have missed entirely if it were not for his keen eye.

When we arrived at Plaza de Argentina, the base camp was mostly deserted. Later there would be hundreds of climbers, but now only a handful of tents sprouted here and there behind their makeshift rock walls. It was early in the season, and the weather was unseasonably cold and windy. After we set up the tents, I constructed a simple small medicine wheel out of stones, the first of four we would place on the mountain to honor the apus. We offered traditional ceremonial gifts of coca leaves from Peru and tobacco from North America and requested a safe journey up the mountain with good weather to make it possible.

At 14,271 feet, base camp was a good place to acclimatize. We would carry everything we needed up the mountain ourselves. On the first day out of base camp, we made a light carry to camp 1, our packs mostly loaded with food, stove fuel, and warm clothing. The rough trail carried us to a craggy valley surrounded by ice fields at 16,240 feet. We had to negotiate a trail among thousands of densely packed *penitentes*, sharp wind-carved ice formations that can rise five feet or more. The route was tortuous, and small stones constantly rolled down from the melting above the trail. We kept a sharp lookout for larger rocks that could become bone-breaking missiles, but we were fortunate to move through unscathed. After the penitentes, the trail coursed over intensely windy and dramatically rocky terrain before becoming sharply steeper upon a large ice field. Here we zigzagged up a very steep section of rock-hard ice covered by a few inches of fresh snow. Several in our group were visibly shaken, terrified by this section of trail, but there was no alternative route and we pressed on. This was simply the challenging nature of the climb.

When the climbing became difficult like this, I remembered my shamanic training to ask the spirit of the mountain for courage and strength. I practiced a chi gong breathing exercise to draw vitality from the mountain with every inhale and to let go of whatever was burdening me with every exhale. This proved beneficial and helped me forget my fears and my fatigue.

We managed the ice field without incident and arrived at camp 1 exhausted but exhilarated when, as if by magic, a white falcon flashed over our heads in a spectacle of speed and beauty. After caching our supplies, we returned to base camp. The treacherous ice field commanded as much attention on the way down as on the way up.

At about this time I began to appreciate how difficult this climb would be. Over the next two days we made two more carries over this same route, but each day the weather and conditions changed, making for dramatically different experiences. The second day hit us with heavy winds and extremely low temperatures and we beat a hasty retreat after setting up a tent at camp 1. The third carry was very challenging because we were carrying full packs of forty-five to fifty pounds through the penitentes and up the steep ice fields. On this day I concentrated on every breathing and mental exercise I had ever learned from my shaman teachers over the years, and to my relief and satisfaction the exercises paid excellent dividends. Despite the hardships, I felt keenly awake and happy to be on this trip. Arriving at our destination, we immediately began the daily process of collecting and melting ice for hydration. At these altitudes, water is frozen unless you are fortunate enough to find a small trickle of running water.

That night an intense storm hit with high winds and subzero temperatures, resulting in wind chills of up to thirty degrees below zero. I registered four degrees in the tent as we cooked dinner from the awkward position of being stuffed in our expedition sleeping bags. Frost from our breath condensed and lined the inside of the tent, turning it into something like an igloo. Every move became slow-motion labor, and keeping warm was the primary objective. Boiling water endlessly, we poured it into our water bottles and stuck them between our legs to keep warm. Unbeknownst to me the water was too hot for my skin, and I woke up with a nasty burn on my thigh that was not to heal for a month. Serious shamanic tests often leave a permanent mark and this is one I will carry with me for the rest of my life.

At these altitudes, skin cracks and scratches and cuticle tears become serious problems because they simply do not heal for lack of oxygen. Eventually all of our fingers and knuckles were covered with medical tape and Band-Aids to protect scratches and cracks that wouldn't mend until we returned to lower elevations. I discovered the value of superglue on skin cracks, and it prevented some of the worst ones. This was all part of the challenge of high-altitude climbing and we took it in stride.

That night for the first time, I had trouble with the altitude and felt as though I were drowning. Laurie advised me to take Diamox, a prescription medication for altitude sickness, and it improved my condition immensely. Some of the others on our team started it too.

The next morning the storm continued unabated and we couldn't escape going out to relieve ourselves. Such an ordinary process becomes extremely trying under such conditions, and I learned to appreciate the luxury of nice sheltered toilets in everyday life. Laurie suggested we return to base camp to get some exercise and escape the fury of the storm.

We made the trip to base camp to find that the older supply tent we had left there had been flattened by the storm. Other climbers' tents had also been destroyed, and the outfitters said the storm had been terrific. All the outhouses had blown down. But returning to base camp gave us the opportunity to have a cooked meal with one of the outfitters as well as access to warm water to wash ourselves and feel more civilized. It was a welcome relief.

At this point TJ announced that he would not be continuing. Trying to do business by satellite phone, he learned that one of his merger deals was not going well and Laurie cautioned him that it was dangerous to have his mind elsewhere and not on the climb. Bill, our other guide, would go back with him to the highway. This meant that Laurie would be our only guide to the top and if something happened to any one of us, we would have to abort the climb. This fact made each of us aware of our responsibility to every other team member. None of us wanted to be the one forcing the trip to end, so from this point onward we were all extra careful and put out an additional effort that ultimately paid off.

The next day, for the fourth time in four days, we climbed up to camp 1, where we were met with an amazing sight. A beautiful hawk was sitting in our camp on a rock next to our tents. Laurie said he had never in all his years seen a hawk in camp there. In our eyes this was a positive and welcome sign that we had approached the mountain with proper respect and protocol.

I thought of the hawk feathers we were carrying with the intention of depositing them on the higher reaches of the mountain.

From here we began our carries to camp 2 at 18,897 feet. The trail rose through another steep ice and snowfield, curved over to a col, and then rose several thousand feet more over rocky terrain in a number of zigzags to camp 2. At these heights the scenery became spectacular with the peerless Andes spread out all around us. The challenge was to pay attention to where we were placing our feet while appreciating the fabulous scenery. At the col the wind suddenly blasted with hurricane force and each step became an exercise in staying balanced under our heavy loads. Higher, we found a rocky perch out of the wind and witnessed a truly spectacular sight. Long fingers of icy clouds coiled out from the peak of Aconcagua, creating an aerial display that none of us had ever witnessed before. The cloud show left us open mouthed and staring in wonder. It was hard to break away and resume the challenge of the climb and again watch our every step. On this trek fingers and toes lost their feeling and the cold wind became a ferocious force sucking the air out of our lungs.

At camp 2 the air was rarified and breathing truly became a challenge. I had never been above seventeen thousand feet and found I could barely catch my breath. Laurie put us right to work preparing a tent site for our high camp, and the labor was absolutely exhausting, but this was the only way to acclimatize. The trick was to put tent stakes into the frozen ground without ever lowering our heads below heart level or we risked passing out.

We built the next of our medicine wheels here on top of the world. Although it had taken us many hours to climb up, going back down to camp 1 was a speedy affair. Laurie demonstrated to us how to move fast on the way down by literally skating down the scree, and we covered all three thousand feet in an hour. Going down was terrifically hard on the knees and thighs, and upon reaching camp 1, I was achingly exhausted. Fair weather saw us through the night and we made another light carry over the same territory the next day, this time in harsher weather.

Finally it was time to carry full packs up to camp 2, a seriously daunting endeavor. I was most concerned about this part of the climb because carrying heavy loads is not my forte. At 140 pounds, I had to heft over a third of my body weight in very thin air and this was extremely difficult for me. This would be a make-or-break affair because if any one of us failed to make the carry, none of us could summit. No one wanted to be the deal breaker so we toughed it out over many hours. To help myself climb, I sang quietly to the apus, something I learned from my Shipibo and Andean shaman teachers in Peru who taught me that to make contact with apus you must sing to them as if you were singing a lullaby to a baby. You must respectfully sing of their great beauty and power and tell them exactly what you want of them. I sang and asked for strength and endurance, which I then felt surging through me as if by magic. There was a point at which I realized I was going to make it, and I felt such a thrill of exhilaration that tears streamed down my face, freezing in seconds in the icy winds. I asked that the others feel the same endurance, fortitude, and strength, and although it was very difficult for some of our party, we all made it. Lena's effort to get to camp 2 was so great that she was hypothermic by the time we got there, so Laurie immediately put her in a sleeping bag in the tent and brewed her cups of hot tea to warm her. The rest of us set up the other tent, melted snow, and cooked dinner in the thin atmosphere. It is common to lose one's appetite at these elevations, but I was starving and was able to eat a big meal. Some in our little group skipped dinner and just crashed.

The next day was supposed to be a rest day, but with Laurie there was no such thing. We spent it acclimatizing and training in new skills. Laurie had us out on the Polish Glacier that looms above camp 2, practicing putting on and taking off our crampons. We got a full class on how to walk like John Wayne to avoid impaling ourselves with our own spikes. He wanted us to take them on and off six times in rapid succession until we knew how to do it by feel in the dark. The weather continued to deteriorate, and before long he had us building cairns to mark our passage up the traverse. The next day was supposed to be summit day but the weather was so bad we had to take a rain check.

Before turning in to the tent, I checked out two graves that were but a stone's throw from our tent. They were simple affairs of piled stone with makeshift crosses made from metal debris. At the foot of one grave was a pair of climbing boot liners attached to feet sticking out of the end of the rock pile, a sobering reminder of the dangers of altitude. Finding some rocks big enough to cover up the feet was a real effort. Afterward I offered some tobacco for this climber and all the climbers who had met their end in this harsh environment. According to Laurie, the graves had been there since the eighties when two helicopters were sent up to help after an accident and both of them crashed, delivering more fatalities. Now the local authorities no longer send help, and some of the climbers who die here are simply buried on the mountain, their bodies too difficult and expensive to bring down.

Two years previously, four Argentinean climbers had perished above camp 2 on the Polish Glacier. They had been roped together but had not anchored themselves to the ice, and so when one slipped they all crashed down the mountain together in a tangle of crampons, rope, packs, and limbs, meeting a grisly and bloody death. Up here in the thin, oxygen-deprived air, climbers don't always think straight and unfortunately they sometimes make serious errors in judgment. One of the most serious of these is underestimating the difficulty of the mountain and continuing for the summit too late in the day so that rescue becomes nearly impossible. The weather can turn from mild to nasty within minutes. Many have perished this way. Several years ago Laurie arrived on the summit to find a frozen corpse of an Argentinean guide lying on his back with one arm extended skyward. He had told his clients he was just going to rest a little and would be joining them in a few minutes. He lay down, probably went to sleep, and never woke up. This is the way altitude sickness can strike, with shocking suddenness and complete mental disability. Here you can never let your guard down for even a moment.

Sobered, I headed for the tent to wait out another fierce mountain storm. In the morning it had mostly abated, and we were able to make a practice summit run. Covering a third of the distance to around twenty thousand feet helped acclimatize us for the effort ahead. This day turned out to be extraordinarily beautiful, and the scenery was peerless in its expansive top-of-the-world views. The Pacific Ocean appeared to the west of Chile. Glaciers, ice fields, and tiers of high mountains rose up to meet the sky in every direction. Mercedario, rising to twenty-two thousand feet, loomed up to the north, a mountain Laurie mentioned he wanted to climb someday.

To prepare for summit day we melted snow and filled all our water bottles with boiling water, prepared our gear and snacks, and then tried to get some sleep because of the early rising time the next morning. Yet sleep was elusive and a heavy wind began its onslaught, making summit day an uncertainty. Fitful and cold, we all moved in and out of disturbed sleep waiting for Laurie's call. The early morning winds became so heavy I was certain we would not be going, but suddenly Laurie's yell pierced the darkness. "Get up! We're leaving in twenty minutes." The wind had strangely abated altogether.

Trying to hurry at nineteen-thousand-plus feet in a small tent in freezing temperatures is extremely difficult. I staggered half asleep out of the tent into the starlight and fixed my crampons to my boots by feel. I thought, *This is it! Crunch time!* But in all truth I felt tired and unready. One of our members was slow to get going and it wasn't until five thirty that we were assembled and on the trail.

We had on every warm item of clothing we owned, including down coats enclosing the hot water bottles. Our headlamps swung this way and that, lighting the cairns we had so carefully constructed over the past couple of days. The dawn revealed itself in unbelievable splendor as we trudged up the long traverse, crunching over snow and ice to connect with the normal route coming from the Plaza de Mulas on the west side. Our route would be much longer than that more popular one. Eventually we intersected that trail and ran into a steady stream of climbers coming up the other side. Some of them had been waiting three weeks for decent weather to summit; finally the time had come. The trail became extraordinarily steep, and climbers could take only three or four steps before resting. At one point I lost all feeling in one of my feet and Laurie made me take off my boot while he massaged life back into it again. Again we set off, rising higher and higher, eventually entering a harsh, windswept gully leading to the summit. Here we met climbers in trouble: a South African with no water; an Australian spitting blood and descending rapidly; a Spaniard suffering from altitude and fatigue, literally crawling his way up the mountain. We offered assistance when possible and continued our upward climb. I lost all track of time and could eventually see climbers at the top and hear them shouting to their fellow climbers below.

Suddenly, and unbelievably, I heard Laurie say. "Well, guys, it's time to turn around." I could see the summit. I could practically touch it. I could smell it. Yet Laurie continued: "It's two thirty, past our turnaround time. Let's go." Laurie, of course, was the boss and the expert.

I tried to evaluate the situation. I felt lightheaded, but for the most part I was in good shape. I could make it but I had to confront the fact that getting to the summit was not the be-all and end-all of the trip. It was the total experience of the climb I had come for. I was on a pilgrimage and had already accomplished the essentials of the weeks-long ceremony. I realized at that moment that to truly understand the priorities of what was important I would not be allowed to summit. The apu had closed that door in order to teach me. I quickly looked around for a spot to make the final medicine wheel and gathered the rocks together. Laurie helped me in silence. I added tobacco and placed the hawk feathers I had brought with me to release on the mountain. Lena and Fred were still coming up the trail, still climbing to where Kathy, Laurie, and I stood. Clearly not feeling well, Lena was dizzy but relentlessly forcing herself up the mountain. Laurie checked on her with concern and said flatly, "Let's go." We prepared to go down, fully understanding that now it was necessary for us to get down fast.

Just as we left our highest point, a golden brown dog with a sweet face and swollen teats approached, coming down from the summit. This was impossible—no one sees dogs at this elevation. Yet here she was, ambling along as if she were on an ordinary walk, apparently feeling no effects from the altitude whatsoever. At first we just gaped at her, uncomprehending. Then she attached herself to our group and with great loyalty accompanied us down the mountain for the rest of the day. We passed many climbers still on their way up the mountain, but we were going down with purpose, Laurie and Fred supporting Lena as we descended. We dropped three thousand feet in a hurry, and Lena began to feel better again. She doesn't remember much about that sequence, just the dog and the power of the mountain. By the time we got back to within sight of camp, it had been twelve hours. I can't remember ever being so tired in my life; Lena was fine but tired too. The dog curled up outside our tent to keep us company, whining pitifully in the cold. We found something for her to eat and called her into our tent, where she snuggled up between us.

Suddenly I had a realization. This was no ordinary dog. Since we had been denied the summit of Aconcagua by five hundred feet, the summit had come to us in the form of this wonderful dog. Aconcagua is a female apu, and of course the dog was female. Lovingly we covered her with a down coat, and we all crashed into deep, exhausted slumber.

The next morning we broke camp and started down, carrying full, heavy packs with everything we had carried up. I thought going down would be easy but it was clearly not a simple task. Navigating the icy slopes with a full pack is treacherous and requires absolute attention. Not a few times I slipped on rocks and ice and terrified myself, but there was nothing to do but get up and keep going. We descended six thousand feet in just a couple of hours. At base camp, after sorting out the things that would go down on mules and those we would carry ourselves, we set off again and dropped another two thousand feet. Our red blood cell count made us feel powerful and energized, and we admired lush green grass and bushes and marveled at the beauty of the landscape we had not fully appreciated on the way up. Out of a desire to carry a light load, we had shed many of our supplies. We slept outside without tents and witnessed the most magnificent display of stars I have ever seen. The night was extremely cold and conducive to active dreaming, but the brown apu dog helped keep us warm once again.

The next day we faced a daunting task. It was more than thirty-five miles to the highway and we had to cover it all by nightfall—without food. I had never walked more than twenty miles in a day, and the trail was extremely rocky and difficult in many places. Keeping a good pace, we covered an amazing amount of ground, yet by about twenty miles our legs were cramping and our toenails were hurting badly. Here, with great gratitude and sad farewells, we left the apu dog with the rangers, hoping she would attach herself to climbers who were going in.

We covered the last fifteen miles in an agonized dream state. When we arrived at the highway to meet the van that would take us back to Mendoza, we were beyond exhaustion. Limping and staggering, I led our little group in a ceremony of thanksgiving for a successful pilgrimage to Aconcagua. By this time everyone fully understood the power of what we had experienced and had great gratitude for returning safely.

In three hours we were in Mendoza, and after welcome hot showers we were out eating a hearty meal that we could only dream of during the last three weeks. After several recovery days in town, Lena and I returned to Santa Fe in time for Christmas Eve with the family.

POSTSCRIPT

I observed several phenomena in retrospect after returning home. For two weeks following the trip, every night was like the night before summit day. Intense dreams marked each night, and every morning I expected Laurie's voice to boom out, "Get up! We're leaving in twenty minutes." I woke up with a sense that I had been traveling extensively all night. Lena and I both felt extremely altered and nothing seemed normal or recognizable. I was certain I would never be quite the same again. I felt the mountain had come back with me to support me and help me. I was not used to this strange feeling. While watching *Lord of the Rings: The Return of the King*, I had a moment of terror when I recognized that the mountain was with me in the theater and was calling to me just as Frodo was climbing up to throw the ring into the lava. I realized it was possible that I could return to climb it again, though this could be done in the dream state as well. Climbing Aconcagua was physically the hardest thing either of us had ever done in our lives, yet it made other endeavors quite possible.

In my assessment over the years, the bid for power on the mountain was successful in every way. I do feel more powerful, more resilient, more willing, and more alive than ever before. I am extremely grateful to have had the opportunity to make this extraordinary climb.

EXERCISE

Get to know a powerful natural totem or ally. Perhaps it is one of your local mountains, a canyon, waterfall, river, pond, or rock formation. Spend some time getting familiar with it and visit it often. Talk to it and perhaps ask it questions. Bring it offerings and blessings. See if it starts to get inside your dreams or thoughts. What is its nature, its qualities, its characteristics? What is its medicine? What does it require of you? What is the price it demands? How can it help you?

15

TRAVERSING THE ANDES AND OTHER POWERFUL PASSAGES

Lena and I met Agustin, a slight, short mestizo curandero, for the first time in Lima, where we arranged for our seven-hour journey by bus into the mountains. We had been corresponding with him by email for a couple of years, but it took a while for us to actually meet him and experience his healing work with the sacred plants of the Andes. Now it was finally happening and we were thrilled.

Agustin introduced Lena and me to the hot springs on the west side of the Andes where we soaked for many hours in an outdoor pool at an elevation of ten thousand feet. He explained that it was possible to take horses from there over a high pass to the eastern side of the Andes and then reach the Stone Forest by bus. Totally intrigued with this promise of grand adventure, we planned a trip for our next two-year program. The trip turned out to be a dream, and after a couple of days soaking in the hot springs, twenty of us hopped on tough mountain ponies for the all-day trek over the Andes. We had to get an early start and were on the trail by 7 A.M. Although some in our group had very little riding experience, everyone did amazingly well.

On our way up over the mountains it sleeted, rained, snowed, and hailed and we took it all in stride. The trail wound through a beautiful valley and then through a steep gorge with waterfalls that got us quite wet. Once up through the gorge, we wove through a long valley with high peaks on either side and hanging glaciers' bright snowfields. Below spread a verdant valley with llamas, alpacas, and the occasional vicuñas. In the afternoon we arrived at the base of a steep section that would take us up to the highest pass at sixteen thousand feet.

After a rest and a snack, up we went through some of the most rugged and beautiful terrain I have ever seen. We arrived at a turquoise mountain lake, threaded around it, and began our ascent of the pass. At one point we dismounted from the horses and let them climb by themselves. We climbed on foot, slowly and panting, to the top of the pass where the views of the Andes were stupendous. Late in the day, the winds were blowing hard and the cold was intense, but everyone was totally invigorated.

Next came terrain of ponds and marshes that we had to navigate to get to the small village where our bus awaited us. Somehow word that we were coming had preceded us and the town had prepared a celebration, a parade in honor of the visitors from another country who had come to their small village. That was when we discovered how rare visitors were here. While we were eager to get to the hot springs, we obliged our hosts and with them politely toasted our visit.

Then we took a two-hour ride in an ancient bus whose floor had been cleaned using diesel fuel. It reeked of the stuff, and the choice was to freeze with the windows open or choke with them shut. We chose to freeze until we couldn't take it anymore.

The ride took us through the Altiplano (high plain) and then into rugged mountains where very big mining operations were under way. The mountains had been gouged out with massive equipment, and construction was going on everywhere we looked. This was painful to see after all the beauty we had enjoyed.

We arrived at the Stone Forest after dark and put up our tents in the intense cold of thirteen thousand feet. Although we sat in a cold open-air room, a warm dinner gave us new life. It was not until the next day that we were treated to the spectacular terrain that is the Stone Forest. Great dragon spines of huge rock came down from the steep sides of the mountains on either side into the valley where we were camping

We discovered we were camped right next to local hot springs with some developed pools that the local miners and their families used. That day we climbed into the maze of rocks above us and conducted an amazing *huachuma* ceremony and enjoyed the thousands of faces of animals, spirits, and characters among the towering rocks. For several hours, each person had the opportunity to wander alone among the castle rocks. Finally a bell called everyone together for the walk back. Huachuma is the ancient medicine that has been used for a documented five thousand years in this part of the Andes. Basically, it is derived from the body of a huge cactus that grows at high elevation and looks similar to the saguaro of Arizona. There is almost no way to describe the experience other than to say that it opens up the mind to higher states of awareness, beautiful light, and expanded intelligence. This medicine is not unlike peyote. During a huachuma ceremony, it is possible to download great wisdom and understanding about the nature of reality and your purpose in being alive.

Upon returning at the end of the day sunburned, tired, and happy, the whole group chose to go into the hot springs pool that contained the entrance to a cave at one end. The cave is long and completely dark, filled with hot water and a rushing cascade at its end. There we reveled for hours, soaking in the hot waters and the dark, talking, laughing, and sharing a wonderful camaraderie. After several days of climbing among the rocks and visiting the hot pools, it was time to return home. We returned to do this trip with every two-year group we had for a number of years, and naturally each trip came with its own unexpected adventures and wonderful discoveries.

Then came the fateful time when we arrived with the Owl group, and of course because they were Owls, many of our adventures happened at night. This time we arrived at our starting point, the first set of hot springs, and soaked for a couple of days before mounting the horses for the trek over the Andes. However, the day of the trek was right after one of Peru's biggest holidays, and unbeknownst to us, all the gauchos were dead drunk by the time we were supposed to leave. Also, only a handful of horses had arrived to take our group of twenty across the Andes.

We wasted hours rounding up enough horses and sober gauchos to make the trip. By the time everything was in place, it was around ten in the morning, very late to set out. But we had very little choice because a bus awaited us on the other side, the luggage with all our tents had already left in a truck, and we couldn't get where we were going any other way. Although we hustled, it was getting dark by the time we arrived at our usual snack place before climbing the pass.

Then it started to rain. As we rode up the pass, it got completely dark. The rain turned to sleet, and problems were beginning to happen. Sixty-eight-year-old Flora had never ridden a horse before except for a little training run. Ben's stirrup broke, sending him flying and breaking a rib. Steve's horse threw him and he screamed so loud we thought he was dying. Among the twenty of us, we had only a few headlamps, but we were told to turn them off because the horses could see better in the dark without them. The gauchos kept yelling to keep track of the donkey that carried some of our supplies. Some of our people were furious that the gauchos seemed more worried about the donkey than about us, but as it turned out, the donkey was the only one who knew the way in the dark. I could not see my hand in front of me over that sixteen-thousand-foot pass, and while I had been keeping track of everyone prior to this, I now had no way of doing so. I was blind like everyone else and simply following voices in the dark. It was every Owl for himself.

As we threaded our way through the marshes, a horse reared and threw its occupant into a pond. Fortunately, she was able to get back on but was now soaked through. As we entered the town in the dark, Brad was knocked off his horse when it struck a wire across the trail, and a little bit later another rider's horse reared up when dogs ran out barking. He crashed to the ground right in front of me and didn't get up for a while. Finally we tied up the horses and crowded into a little store that sold crackers and things. I looked around with grave concern. Thank God we were all accounted for, but as I looked around I saw bloody faces, tears, torn clothes, exhaustion, wet boots and raincoats, and intense shivering in the cold. I heard groans and whimpering and the chattering of teeth. Townspeople brought us blankets and hot drinks and we were ever so grateful.

To make matters worse, the bus had left, the driver thinking we were not coming because it was so late. Eventually the bus was called back and we had to wait a long time for it to arrive. Damned Owls—everything in the dark. The ride was a somber affair. No one had the energy to even talk; there were just huge sighs and more groaning. I was really worried. This adventure had gone very badly, and I felt completely responsible. I was sure no one would ever want to go on a trip with us again, much less continue this program. I just hoped everyone would recover from their injuries and that no one would die of hypothermia.

When we arrived at the hot springs, it was very cold and I could not imagine everyone setting up tents and sleeping in them. Fortunately, Agustin had called ahead and arranged for us to stay in a new building there. It had a fireplace with a crackling blaze, and a hot meal awaited us. Then everyone spread out on the floor and went to sleep. There was much snoring that night.

The next morning Lena and I decided to have a big check-in to see how everyone was faring. I was prepared for the worst. I figured at the very least we would get yelled at. We got in a big circle and each person spoke. As we went around, my chagrin turned to amazement. People were laughing, excited, telling war stories. Flora, our oldest member who I thought would die, was smiling brightly and said she'd just had the best day of her life. Others who were hobbling around with sticks said they wouldn't trade the experience for the world. Lena and I were stunned.

Some people like an adventure gone bad more than any other kind; they get to feel their mortality. The Owls had survived. They showed themselves they could come through something very difficult and live to tell about it. It was a victory, and of course they knew it had to be done in the dark. In short, this was a massive bid for power and they knew it.

The next day we did our traditional huachuma ceremony and it was truly amazing. Some of our people could not navigate so well because they were hurting from the harsh journey, so they just found a good spot and settled down with the medicine and enjoyed the hell out of it. Others, sailing on the high of their survival, went deeper than ever before into their own sense of empowerment and discovery of the strength within. The day was filled with awe, laughter, smiles, and deep contentment.

Although years have gone by, the veterans from this trip still regale others with the tale of their trip across the Andes and what an amazing ordeal it was. As I look back I just shake my head and marvel at how things work out even in the direst circumstances.

On a poignant note, Cathy, one of the most vocal about how amazing her trip was, died several weeks later of sudden-onset pancreatitis. When she was in the hot springs she shouted out, "I love all you. You are all my family." We had no notion that very soon she would no longer be with us. In retrospect I now know why she came on that trip. She had been going through some very difficult times: a divorce and other big challenges. At some level we all know we are going to die and she wanted to do something extraordinary before she did. She was also able to let us all know how much she cared for us before she went. As it turns out, one of our group saw Cathy's death coming during the huachuma ceremony. She said she just knew but did not know exactly when it would be. It turned out to be sooner than she expected.

Cathy was a heart surgery nurse—an extremely stressful occupation. Some months before this trip she called me and told me that a good friend of hers, a doctor, had dropped dead of a heart attack while performing surgery. She wanted to process this experience with me and I obliged her. A couple of weeks after we returned home, I went to San Diego to pick up Enrique and Herlinda, who were arriving from Peru. We did a couple of ceremonies together in Encinitas, and as I was walking out of the house in the morning, a fair-sized bird suddenly fell out of the sky dead at my feet. I looked up and saw no wires, branches, or obstacles overhead, just clear sky. Instantly I knew someone was going to die; I just did not know who.

I drove Enrique and Herlinda back to Santa Fe and on the way received the news that Cathy had gone into the hospital. Now, Cathy had been to the jungle with us a number of times, and she loved Herlinda and Enrique. So I flew with Enrique to Phoenix, rented a car, and drove to the hospital where Cathy had worked and was now a patient. She was unconscious and had endless machines wired up to her. Enrique and I went to work doing what healing we could in the hospital setting, trying not to interfere with the machines. Enrique and I looked at each other, and we silently communicated with our eyes that we knew she was going. All we could do was help prepare her. I sat next to her for a long time with my eyes closed, and she confirmed that she was exiting this life and it was her chosen time. Enrique and I returned that evening to Santa Fe, and a few days later she was gone.

Although I accepted her choice, it was hard because I had just come through such an adventure with her and saw her at the peak of life. You never know what is going to happen next.

I have come to the conclusion that some people who are attracted to the shamanic path want to use it as preparation for leaving this life. This is not a bad thing, since other than Tibetan Buddhism, religion does not usually prepare people for death very well. Shamanism is comfortable with death and handles it as a rite of passage or state of transition. Thus, some people want to get comfortable with making a transition before choosing on an essence level to do so. Most mature and older souls don't want to view their death as some kind of failure. They want to see it as a natural transition after learning the lessons of self-acceptance or after having the realization that they are loved after all.

POSTSCRIPT

Sometimes the hardest experiences in life turn out to be the most revitalizing and empowering. One important lesson is to never jump to conclusions about what other people are experiencing. Death sometimes does come suddenly, like a thief in the night. Yet it is never an accident. There are always little signs and warnings along the way. Sometimes it comes with the announcement that one finally feels really and truly loved. That is what Cathy came to learn, and that is where she chose to transfer out. Death is always powerful.

EXERCISE

Think back to a difficult experience that pushed you to your limits: physically, emotionally, and psychologically. Perhaps you thought you were not going to get through it, but then you found the extra strength to navigate it and were able to reach the other side. What warrior actions were required of you? What leader-like responsibilities did you need to take on? How did you manage to find clarity in a confusing, challenging event?

IN CLOSING

When I first decided to write these stories down, I looked forward to great enjoyment revisiting the many remarkable places and events I have chronicled here. That is exactly what happened, but so much more took place as well. Little did I know that it would be a major experience of healing and completion for me. In recalling these stories, I have had the opportunity to learn an amazing amount that I had previously failed to see. Many of these experiences brought me to tears, not once but each time I read them over. Perhaps some of these stories have affected you in the same way. Whatever the case, I had the opportunity to grieve in ways I did not at the time and to feel enormous gratitude for the experience, even if it was sad or painful. There were also stories that made me laugh out loud or chuckle every time I went over them. Over and over again I experienced the big three: Gratitude, Love, and Awe, the three vibrations that fertilize the seed of awakening. As my students all know, they form the acronym GLA, a silly non-word that I use as slang to reference the road to self-realization.

These stories represent only a tiny fraction of the numerous adventures of my life but in many ways these are the ones I like to tell the most. None of these stories is from my childhood. I have many of those but I chose not to dwell on them in this book; they are perhaps for a different volume of stories to be told another time. Maybe I left them for later because they are very painful and I am still healing from them. I did have my share of magic as a child but this was often overshadowed by difficult events, difficult people, a high degree of sensitivity, dysfunctional family patterns, and great frustration. That set of stories, when I tell them, may be even more healing than these.

It is my wish that you were entertained by these stories and that you learned something of value from them for your own process. You see, in many ways these stories are as much yours as they are mine. I truly believe that the refined virtual reality experience that is my life is also part of everyone's experience because in the end, when the games are over, we are all one. Your stories are mine and mine are yours, so you can learn what you need to. In the end they are the dreams of either a lunatic or a very wise old soul. Take your pick. Or then again, perhaps they are both.

Many Blessings on your journey, from one adventure traveler to another.

José Luis Stevens

ACKNOWLEDGMENTS

Several people were particularly instrumental in helping me write this book.

Thanks to one of my high school English teachers, who I shall not name. Some years ago at my fortieth high school reunion, I approached him and thanked him profusely for helping me become a good writer. He responded with a look of utmost disagreeableness and said something shockingly insulting and off-putting. I was completely stunned. Only later did I realize what emotional pain he was in and that he had learned to deal with that pain by teaching others to write well.

I thank him again, and maybe one day he will be able to feel my gratitude in his heart.

Thanks to Sheridan McCarthy, my editor contracted through Sounds True. She was tasked with an enormous challenge: to cut, cut, cut the manuscript down by thousands of words. Through her careful and sensitive touch she managed to avoid cutting the essence, just eliminating the unnecessary, and for that I am very grateful.

Thank you to Kay Kamala, who first read my rather massive transcript and gave me sound advice.

Much gratitude to Mitchell Clute from Sounds True and to Tucker Collins for also reading my original manuscript and giving me most valuable feedback.

ABOUT THE AUTHOR

José Luis Stevens, PhD, is an international lecturer, teacher, consultant, and trainer. A psychologist, licensed clinical social worker, and author of twenty books and ebooks, as well as numerous articles, he is also on the board of the Society for Shamanic Practice. He is the cofounder of the Power Path School of Shamanism and the Center for Shamanic Education and Exchange. He completed a ten-year apprenticeship with a Huichol maracame and has studied extensively with the Shipibos of the Amazon and the Q'ero of the Andes for the past twenty-five years.

He has a doctorate in integral counseling from the California Institute of Integral Studies, a master's degree in clinical social work from the University of California, Berkeley, and a bachelor's degree in sociology from Santa Clara University, California.

He lives in Santa Fe, New Mexico, with his wife and task companion, Lena.

Contact information:
    Website: www.thepowerpath.com
    Email: admin@thepowerpath.com
    Office phone: (505) 982-8732

ABOUT SOUNDS TRUE

Sounds True is a multimedia publisher whose mission is to inspire and support personal transformation and spiritual awakening. Founded in 1985 and located in Boulder, Colorado, we work with many of the leading spiritual teachers, thinkers, healers, and visionary artists of our time. We strive with every title to preserve the essential "living wisdom" of the author or artist. It is our goal to create products that not only provide information to a reader or listener, but that also embody the quality of a wisdom transmission.

For those seeking genuine transformation, Sounds True is your trusted partner. At SoundsTrue.com you will find a wealth of free resources to support your journey, including exclusive weekly audio interviews, free downloads, interactive learning tools, and other special savings on all our titles.

To learn more, please visit SoundsTrue.com/freegifts or call us toll-free at 800.333.9185.